Another "marriage book"?! Yes and no. Yes, a book on marriage, but no, not just "another" book on marriage. In it, Danny and Amy DeWalt take you on a fast-paced and hard-hitting journey beyond the expected behaviors and practices for a good marriage. With deep integrity from D———— ————— ory of marital redemption, this book exposes who ‌ tack marriages and shows how your marriage c‌ and freedom. I promise that if you engage hone ‌ ook . . . well, just do it and see what happens. I ‌ , and this book to you!

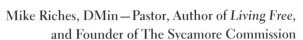

Mike Riches, DMin—Pastor, Author of *Living Free*, and Founder of The Sycamore Commission

Like great mechanics, Danny and Amy not only give a helpful, biblical diagnostic for a healthy marriage, but also outline a number of practical exercises to tune up your relationship. Full of practical advice and story, this book gets to the heart of the matter of what makes unified relationships last. If you are in need of a no-nonsense manual as to how great relationships function and a step-by-step guide to helping you get there, getting this book would be a solid investment!

Steve Haas—Vice President/Chief Catalyst, World Vision

Danny and Amy are not going green on this one. This is not a book about how to economize in your marriage. It's about laying down some rubber, spinning the wheels, and getting somewhere that Jesus said is worth going together. This book is not for moped riders either. It's not about peddling harder by yourself with a little help from an underpowered engine. Instead, you are invited to the flat tracks to see what a marriage guided by biblical principles can really do. Danny and Amy have nailed it in a vulnerable, insightful, and no-seatbelts book which poses the question for each of our marriages: "Why not red-line it?"

Bob Goff—President and Founder, Restore International

Anyone who wants to reignite, strengthen, or save their marriage needs to read and engage in High Octane Marriage. My wife Jane and I have walked with Danny and Amy for the last 20 years. We have seen them live this book and teach others how to live it as well—us included. High Octane Marriage will take you down a road that may challenge and push you beyond your comfort level—but if you stay on it, the result will be unity with your spouse you never dreamed possible.

David Duea—President and CEO, HopeSparks Family Services

Quite simply, Danny and Amy's teaching is the best marriage training we have ever experienced. It has transformed not only our own relationship, but also our parenting and family life—just ask our five kids! Superb, biblical, and highly practical— Danny and Amy live what they teach.

Silas and Annie Crawley—Pastors of Hope Chapel,
Bristol, United Kingdom

The truths in this book were a life-saver for our marriage. I had it so backwards. Ministry came first and our marriage was subject to whatever ministry demanded. By putting top priority on our marriage, we experienced God's favor in exponential ways. His and her things, which previously permeated our marriage, went out the window and true unity was born. This included ministry which took on a whole new and exciting look as we did it together. What an absolutely life-changing process this has been for our marriage.

Scott and Kindra Mitchell, Executive Pastor, Harborview Fellowship

High Octane Marriage *will no doubt challenge the alignment of your marriage with the truth of God's "original design" for marriage. Lived out, its twelve chapters will take your marriage on a ride you will never forget. Chapter 11—"Breaking the Power of the Secret"—was one of those chapters I thought was written about ME. How could Danny know all those things about me? You could overlay the chapter on my life before freedom and it would line up perfectly. I asked Danny if he had been living in my house. It was so Holy Spirit-directed!*

Robert J., USA

I believe that the true value of anything is seen in its "before and after." This is what my father said to me after I had learned and applied the truths in High Octane Marriage: *"I don't totally understand all of the things you've learned, but I do know this—you are a way better father and husband than you were before."*

John P., USA

God's ordained roles for marriage are the real deal! True joy came when we chose to live in alignment with His truth. Danny and Amy do an excellent job of portraying and teaching these truths. The simple yet powerful principles outlined in High Octane Marriage *have helped us live out "life to the fullest" in our marriage. We'll never be the same!*

BJ and Jennie Q., USA

What makes High Octane Marriage *different from other marriage books is the unique emphasis on repentance and forgiveness—so powerful! The power of forgiveness has softened my heart to receive my husband's love and leadership. I trust Jesus to lead my husband and the stronghold of control has been broken in my life. Thank you, Jesus!*

Phyllis P., USA

High Octane Marriage *is both practical AND spiritually powerful. Previously, we had focused purely on practical tools within our marriage like effective communication and resolving conflict. But, as we discovered, the issues and tensions that constantly play out in a marriage are never fully resolved until we deconstruct the spiritual dynamics lying behind them. Learning to "live in the light" was such a great exercise. We brought things into the light which we hadn't before—and that increased our intimacy as a result!*

Alastair and Fiona S., United Kingdom

We thought we had a really good relationship—but had no idea how good it COULD be until we applied the truths of this book to our marriage. We have discovered and embraced our God-given roles. We've learned to submit to one another and encourage one another into who the Lord created us to be. We are better parents. We have more joy, more love, and are more passionate about our marriage than ever—pretty awesome after 25 years of marriage!

Larry and Lisa G., USA

So many Christian couples have never intimately prayed together. We were one of them until we learned the truths in this book. Now our marriage is transformed through the power of intimate prayer.

Tane and Angie C., USA

Danny and Amy's approach to marriage is both inspirational and refreshing. They teach simple truths in a way that is clear, accessible, and incredibly powerful. We have seen our relationship transformed as a result.

Ben and Joe W., United Kingdom

Our marriage is stronger and healthier since we have put these truths into practice . . .

Brad and Cindy N., USA

Danny and Amy's teaching on submission by GOD'S design radically altered my understanding of my role as a wife. It has brought a peace to me and to my marriage that I didn't know was possible.

Kelly Anne S., USA

I have experienced huge freedom by coming to understand and embrace trust in the Lord toward my husband and his leadership, knowing it is God whom I am ultimately trusting. I have learned to pray for my husband rather than evaluate and try to mold him.

Jane D., USA

Getting into alignment with God's design for our marriage has completely transformed us as a couple and as a family. When conversations begin turn to negative and divisive, we now have the tools stop the downward spiral and fix ourselves on the Lord. "Stop, pray, and get the issue out in front of you. Don't let it divide you." We have seen our marriage and those of our closest friends saved by the practical application of these truths.

Ryan and Margaret R., USA

High Octane Marriage

Danny & Amy DeWalt

SYCAMORE™ PUBLICATIONS

High Octane Marriage: Experience the Power of God's Design
First Edition Trade Book, 2011
Copyright © 2011 by Danny & Amy DeWalt

Additional books can be purchased through The Sycamore Commission (www.sycamorecommission.org) or at www.amazon.com.

Published by Sycamore Publications^SM, LLC. PO Box 158, Gig Harbor, WA 98335. Additional books can be purchased through The Sycamore Commission.

Cover photo used by permission of Ducati North America, All Rights Reserved.

To Order:
www.sycamorecommission.org
info@sycamorecommission.org

ISBN softcover: 978-0-9828756-1-2
ISBN hardcover: 978-0-9828756-2-9
Editorial: Arlyn Lawrence, InPrint Communications, Gig Harbor, WA
Book Packaging: Scribe Book Company, Lawton, OK
Cover Design: Susan Browne, Nashville, TN
Book Design: PerfecType, Nashville, TN
Photography: Larry Godt
Printed in the USA by Color House Graphics, Grand Rapids, MI

First Edition Trade Book, 2011
Copyright © 2011 by Danny & Amy DeWalt

TABLE OF CONTENTS

ABOUT THE AUTHORS

Danny DeWalt is a lawyer, pastor, counselor, and sports enthusiast! He obtained his undergraduate degree in Psychology and Philosophy at California State University, Bakersfield, a Master of Divinity from Princeton Theological Seminary, a Master of Arts in Marriage and Family Therapy from Pacific Lutheran University, and a Juris Doctor from California Western School of Law. Amy DeWalt obtained her liberal arts degree from Evergreen State College with an emphasis in counseling. They both agree with Tony Campolo that one's testimony is far more valuable than one's titles but they also understand that people want to know an author's credentials and so provide those here. Danny is also on the board of the Sycamore Commission and has led conferences and training for couples from around the world.

Danny and Amy have been working with marriages and families for over twenty years. Danny works full-time as a lawyer and is a member of the pastoral team at Harborview Fellowship where he leads marriage and family ministries. Amy has enjoyed the blessing of managing their home and pouring time and energy into their daughters. She has worked extensively ministering to women in the community and from abroad.

They have two young adult daughters, Hannah and Jenna, who have occupied their main attention these past twenty years and brought great joy and humor to their family. Danny and Amy love to play sports, travel, and find adventure wherever they can. They have developed deep friendships around the world and enjoy the richness of hanging out with good friends.

ACKNOWLEDGMENTS

Jesus saved us and our marriage. He faithfully forges His truths in us continually. It is by His grace and His favor that this book could be written. Jesus alone gets all the glory and honor and praise for any healing the truths in this book may bring, for this book finds its roots in His healing hands in our lives. It was commissioned by Him and it is offered humbly for Him.

I know of no other person who more thoroughly and graciously embodies the truths in this book than my wife, Amy. She is a picture of peace and joy and grace. She takes my breath away. Although I have written most of the pages, I would have nothing to say without her. She is the love of my life. She is the backbone of strength in my life. And her decision to pick me was the greatest victory my life will know. This book is our work together and our lives poured out at the feet of Jesus. Sweetie, I am grateful to you and for you above all.

Our fabulous daughters, Hannah and Jenna, have been a central part of our family team in reaching out and ministering to other families from the time they were little. Many of their relationships and influence have led to marriage restoration opportunities. Their endless encouragement and support of our marriage restoration work have made our ministry a total team effort, and their own life stories have provided countless humorous examples that we use with other families, which they generously tolerate.

Jason and Cari Black, Dave and Jane Duea, Larry and Lisa Godt, and John and Phyllis Payne have chosen to travel this adventure with us these past twenty years and most of the materials in this book were formed in the bunkers of blood, sweat, and tears as each of these families navigated together the challenges of life. We are eternally grateful for the love and commitment that these couples have poured into us—not to mention the forbearance of all our mistakes along the way. Thankfully, there has been no shortage of laughs to get us through. Also, thank you to Tane and Angie Cabe for fearlessly jumping in to these truths and teaching us all what it looks like to be real (and thank you, Tane, for the title idea "High Oc*tane*").

My law partner and friend, Bob Goff, required me to make ministry part of my job description 10 years ago. It was out of that generous and passionate vision that our marriage and family ministry took wings. Since that time I am daily inspired by Bob's faith, humor, and go-for-it mission which he lives out in outrageous and audacious ways every day. Most of the things I am involved in, he wrangled me into. Our work in Africa through Restore International—that was Bob. My Ducati motorcycle—that was Bob. It should be clear that the High Octane DNA of this book was largely influenced by Bob and his unique and profound influence in my life.

Mike Riches and Tom Jonez are my pastors, mentors, and friends. They are responsible for receiving the revelation and subsequently developing the truths which form the foundation of this book. And they are responsible for the development of these truths in my life and marriage. They have taken on the frontline position of leading in these Jesus Ministry truths around the world and they have forged the path for couples like us to follow. Most profoundly, they live out the simple truths of Jesus and the fruit of their lives and ministries confirms it. I thank them here for taking a grip on me and never letting go. True friends.

There is an entire community of couples who have endured with patience all of the learning we have gone through this past decade in the development of these materials. The couples of Harborview Fellowship dared to put their marriages into the fires of restoration while we were seeking to understand God's heart and truth and design for marriage. We are so thankful for their work ethic and teachable hearts and we are so thankful to see the fruit in their marriages that God has grown.

Finally, Arlyn Lawrence has chosen to make this project her own. She has poured her life, passion, gifts, and marriage into this book. She has taken raw material and made it something to be proud of. She has provided great guidance and counsel with grace and enthusiasm. She has selflessly deposited in these pages her wisdom and experience with training in Jesus Ministry truths and her passion for marriages and families. We would have never completed this project without Arlyn and her energy and excitement to see it through. Thank you, Arlyn. You are a wonderful gift to our family.

Arlyn introduced us to Dan and Ang DePriest, Susan Browne, and Kristin Goble who made this book come to life with their gifts of publishing and design. We are hugely indebted to your heartfelt investment in this book.

Thank you, Lord for Your truth and the fantastic team and the exhilarating ride that lives behind these pages.

PREFACE

■ ARE YOU READY FOR THE RIDE OF YOUR LIFE?

It will help you to understand the content of this course if you know a bit about me. So sit down and hold on—here it goes . . .

I like fast and I like fun. I like high performance. I like power. I like motorcycles and Porsches. Never had a Porsche but I like them. I like really cold beer and basketball. I also like football, baseball, tennis, and golf. I like playing just about anything on a team, with a group of guys who just want to go for it—full on. I like roller coasters and adrenaline and the exhilaration of letting go. That's my design.

I hate apologizing for what I like. I hate justifying who I am. I hate toning down my passion for cool stuff just because it might tweak someone else. I hate mediocrity. I hate wasting time.

I love my wife. Everything about her. I love the things she loves. I hate the things she hates. She is perfect for me. I love the ways she is different from me. I love what she brings out in me. She loves peace and quiet. She loves joy and laughter. She loves animals and babies.

I hate our culture's portrayal of marriage. I hate the divorce rate. I hate that there are fatherless homes. I hate discouragement and passivity. I hate unforgiveness. I hate withholding. I think God hates that stuff, too.

I love Jesus. I love the Truth. I love true freedom. I love God's design. I love that God designed marriage and that His design is perfect. I love seeing couples get into alignment with God's design. I love it when God's power takes over a marriage and restores it. I love it when it's fast and furious freedom from old patterns and deep wounds.

God likes fast and fun. Consider the speed of light; He created that. God likes power; just look at the wind and the waves. God loves surprising people with joy; look what Jesus did every day—and still does.

Amy and I wrote this book out of our life experiences, best characterized as a journey from arrogance to crisis to brokenness to humility to revelation to transformation to victory and life in the power of God's design. We wrote it for couples like us, who aren't perfect but who want to experience the fullness of God's design for their lives and their marriages. The only way we know how to get there is with a go-for-it, all-out sprint for a high octane marriage.

Join us, if you dare, on the ride of your life. Buckle up, let go, and experience the joy and thrill of alignment with God's design. It will be a high octane ride, guaranteed!

We will hit the road of life full throttle and develop a high octane capacity to navigate the curves, obstacles, mountains, and valleys that life throws at us. Each chapter will be full of biblical truth, real-life stories, and "time to drive" practical exercises to help you and your spouse apply what you're learning and get to real change through spiritual transaction.

So that's the plan. If you are willing to take up the above challenges, then in the pages to follow you will surely encounter the Living God and His crazy favor. You will meet the sweetheart that God designed for you and you will experience life in the Kingdom—which is just too good for words.

Danny DeWalt
Gig Harbor, WA
January 2011

Designed
for Power

igh octane gas (or "petrol," if you're reading this in Europe) is a fuel less likely to cause your engine to knock or ping. Knock, also known as "detonation," occurs when part of the fuel-air mixture in one or more of your car's cylinders ignites spontaneously due to compression, independent of the combustion initiated by the spark plug. When that happens, instead of a controlled burn, you get what amounts to an explosion—not a good thing for your engine! To avoid this, high-octane fuel is formulated to burn slower than regular gas or petrol, making unwanted explosions or detonations less likely, or even non-existent.

No unwanted explosions. Just a smooth, exhilarating, high power drive. That's great for cars—and also a good plan for an increasingly accelerating "high octane" marriage!

Unfortunately, especially when it comes to relationships, people many times feel stuck and powerless to change their situation. On the one hand, we *are* indeed powerless because, in and of ourselves, we have no power to effect real and lasting change. However, as followers of Jesus Christ we know the One who *does* have power—and He shares it with us! Yet so many of us either don't believe we have God's power or don't know how to access it for real acceleration; either way, we feel powerless.

God moves in power: power over death, power over disease, power over demonic influence, and power over discouragement. And that very real power *is* available to us. This section of the book is designed to draw a roadmap for the release of God's power in our lives and marriages. In these four chapters we will learn and apply the truths that unlock the thrill of God's "high octane" power moving us toward transformed lives and marriages, truths such as:

Original Design
Alignment
Brokenness
Submission
Engagement
Exercising Your Authority in Christ

These truths, when applied whole-heartedly, will change your life forever!

CHAPTER ONE

Original Design

For we are God's masterpiece.
He has created us anew in Christ Jesus,
so that we can do the good things he planned for us long ago.

EPHESIANS 2:10

I remember the first time I laid eyes on an Audi TT convertible sports car. I almost got into an accident because I couldn't stop looking at it. I actually turned around and chased it just to get a longer look. It just looked fast and fun! I thought we would probably get along great.

There is nothing that can match a beautiful design. A beautiful design is a piece of art. In fact, the Audi TT is one of the only cars ever displayed at the Guggenheim Museum in New York for timeless design. A true beauty.

God's designs are equally beautiful—even more so since He is the Original Designer. When Amy and I first learned the truth of God's original design for marriage, we were amazed that such a simple truth could be so life changing. Of course, we had always heard people say, "God has a plan for your life." After all, that's the first of the "Four Spiritual Laws." But our scenario was different. We were surviving but not thriving. Amy and I were unaware of how much our history, pain, and wounds were holding us back. We needed more than just the comfort of knowing God had a "plan." We needed a dramatic revelation of God's vision for our lives and marriage.

Then Amy and I discovered the truth of God's original design. We learned about His plan for marriage, and also for us as individuals and as a couple. We found that the Scriptures are full of confirmation that God designed each one of us with a unique design and purpose. His blueprints for His children include design elements that are true about all of us, and elements that are distinctive to each of us.

Once Amy and I understood our individual original designs and how far out of alignment we were living, and then understood God's design for marriage and how far out of alignment our marriage was, we began to catch the vision of God's truth. We got a renewed vision for how God made us and sees us, a vision we knew to be true about each of us and each other. Our problem was that we had forgotten. We had forgotten who we really were. But once reminded of that truth it resonated deep inside and changed us forever. Our whole posture changed toward each other and we began to really affirm and encourage each other. It was the revelation of God's original design that cleared the way for us to get into alignment. It was the revelation of a lifetime!

It is our hope and prayer that you, too—along with your spouse—will have a similar revelation of God's love and marvelous design for you and your marriage. Throughout this book I will continually refer to and highlight many of the design elements that comprise God's original design for *you*. Specifically, we will be exploring how that design relates to marriage, and to *your* marriage in particular.

What do I mean by that? An "original design" element that would be true of all of us, for example, is that God created us to be confident and faith-filled. We were *not* created with a spirit of *fear*:

2 Timothy 1:7

For God has not given us a spirit of fear and timidity, but of power, love, and self-discipline.

In this passage, the Apostle Paul confirms that fear is not part of our original design. God did not make us to be fearful. Jesus frequently said things like, "Do not be afraid" (Mt. 10:26) and "You have so little faith" (Mt. 6:30, 8:26). God designed ALL of us to live by faith and not by fear.

Operating in fear—or any other untruth—puts us out of alignment with God's design. Fear is not found anywhere in God's truth. It is operating in *faith* that brings us into alignment with God's design for our lives. Unpacking this concept of original design further still, I have come to understand that God's original design IS synonymous with the truth. Things like fear (or hopelessness, laziness, shame, etc.) are not the truth about who we are; they are lies that derive their origins from the forces that oppose God. They are crafted to trick and deceive God's children out of understanding and operating in God's powerful, life-giving design for their lives and marriages.

Granted, there are thousands of books out there that talk about how to improve your marriage. But as Amy and I have discovered, there is only one Book that claims to define the non-negotiable road markers established for marriage by the Creator of marriage itself. God's design is the one we are interested in. Lining up with God's truth about how each marriage partner ought to operate is the only way to experience a high octane marriage.

■ God Designed Marriage

Marriage, as God originally designed it, rocks! It is a big deal. It is the foundation of society. Families emerge from a marriage. Communities and tribes are built upon families and nations are formed out of communities. However, when this design breaks down, God's design for creation is compromised. Entire societies break down when the communities, families, and marriages that comprise them are compromised. On the other hand, when there is alignment with God's design, then God's creation flourishes. So it goes with marriages.

The Bible tells us that God had an original design not just for creation in general, but also for specific aspects of his creation—including individual people.[1] He had a plan that was good and perfect, and designed to give us a glorious life in divine relationship with Him—a Kingdom Life. God's original design is *the truth* about His creation.

Genesis 1:26-31

Then God said, "Let us make people in our image, to be like ourselves. They will be masters over all life—the fish in the sea, the birds in the sky, and all the livestock, wild animals, and small animals." So God created people in his own image; God patterned them after himself; male and female he created them. God blessed them and told them, "Multiply and fill the earth and subdue it. Be masters over the fish and birds and all the animals." And God said, "Look! I have given you the seed-bearing plants throughout the earth and all the fruit trees for your food. And I have given all the grasses and other green plants to the animals and birds for their food." And so it was. Then God looked over all he had made, and he saw that it was excellent in every way.

Excellent in every way! I love that. Like a high performance vehicle, God created us in His own image, patterned us after Himself, and made us excellent in every way. God's design reflected God's character and glory, authority, and power. The Scriptures go on to explain that God gave us life by His very own breath: *"And the LORD God formed a man's body from the dust of the ground and breathed into it the breath of life. And the man became a living person. Then the LORD God planted a garden in Eden, in the east, and there he placed the man he had created"* (Gen. 2:7-8).

As soon as God created man, He provided clear parameters for the execution and maintenance of His design. He knew what was best for His creation. He knew that the radical joy He designed for His children could only be experienced through radical obedience, protecting them inside the boundaries that governed His design.

■ The Blueprints

Take a minute with me, before we go on with the story, to think about what a "design" entails. Think about cars again, for example. As an auto designer excitedly develops a new design that has formed in his mind, the design doesn't remain there (in his mind, that is). In order for the car to be properly constructed, the designer must communicate the details of his vision for it. This usually takes place in two ways.

First, the designer creates drawings so that the objective is clear, visible, and apparent. These are the blueprints of the design, which the designer then gives to the auto maker to communicate the details of the design. Second, the designer and the auto maker operate together in the construction of the automobile. In this process, the designer is able to clarify, emphasize, and provide additional details and information for the proper construction of the car.

This is a helpful illustration for understanding "original design" because God uses a similar process to communicate His original design for each of us individually, as well as for our marriages. He has given us His blueprints in the Bible. They are clear, visible, and apparent. He also collaborates with us through His Holy Spirit to communicate more specific information and details about His design for our lives (see John 14:16-17).

Let's look at some biblical examples of original design. In Judges chapter 6, God spoke to Gideon about his original design:

Judges 6:12-16

The angel of the LORD appeared to him and said, "Mighty hero, the LORD is with you!"

"Sir," Gideon replied, "if the LORD is with us, why has all this happened to us? And where are all the miracles our ancestors told us about? Didn't they say, 'The LORD brought us up out of Egypt'? But now the LORD has abandoned us and handed us over to the Midianites."

Then the LORD turned to him and said, "Go with the strength you have and rescue Israel from the Midianites. I am sending you!"

"But Lord," Gideon replied, "how can I rescue Israel? My clan is the weakest in the whole tribe of Manasseh, and I am the least in my entire family!"

The LORD said to him, "I will be with you. And you will destroy the Midianites as if you were fighting against one man."

Notice that God sent an angel to Gideon to awaken him to his original design. At the time of the angel's appearance, Gideon was threshing wheat in an underground cave because he was afraid of being discovered by his enemies. The angel said to him, "*Mighty hero . . .*"

At the time, Gideon looked like anything but a mighty hero. In addition, Gideon didn't recognize or accept those words of original design. He did not even see them in himself. Notice that he responded, "*How can I rescue Israel? My clan is the weakest . . . and I am the least in my entire family!*"

It is important to understand that what God says about us is true whether we know it, see it, or accept it. If you continue reading in Judges, you will see that God's words came true when Gideon finally accepted them and operated in them. The supporting components of Gideon's original design of being a mighty hero were leadership, courage, vision, faith, and obedience. That is who God made Gideon to be. But it wasn't until Gideon became aware of his original design that he was able to choose to live it out.

That is why discovering our original design is a top priority. That is why speaking original design is so important. We need to be made aware of it. We need a revelation from God about it.

Let's look at another example:

Matthew 16:18-19

Now I say to you that you are Peter, and upon this rock I will build my church, and all the powers of hell will not conquer it. And I will give you the keys of the Kingdom of Heaven. Whatever you lock on earth will be locked in heaven, and whatever you open on earth will be opened in heaven.

Here Jesus gives Simon a new name—Peter—and He gives Peter a critical role in the Kingdom. Jesus reveals Peter's true identity—his original design. Notice the supporting components of Peter's original design contained in this passage: rock, strength, power, authority, jurisdiction. Notice that Jesus spoke these things and revealed these things before Peter betrayed him. Notice that Peter's choices and responses to life's circumstances and sin did not change his original design. Peter did become the rock that Jesus revealed. But he had to choose to accept that design and get into alignment with it.

Original design is something that is revealed by God. When we are in touch with the truth of how God made someone, we can help him or her discover God's revelation of his (or her) original design. Original design is not just personality. Personality can be shaped by life and circumstances; it can be positive or negative, interesting or annoying. It is not necessarily grounded in the truth. Original design is only grounded in the truth and it may or may not be seen in someone's life.

There is one other distinction about original design that I would like to make. The Bible speaks to two degrees of original design—general and personal. The examples I gave of Gideon and Peter were examples of *personal* original design. Those words were not spoken as general indicators of God's design for all his children. They were uniquely given to Gideon and Peter.

An example of God's *general* original design is found in Ephesians 2. What we mean by general original design is that those particular words and truths apply to all of God's children, such as, "*For we are God's masterpiece. He has created us anew in Christ Jesus, so that we can do the good things he planned for us long ago*" (Eph. 2:10). This text affirms generally that we are all God's masterpiece. That applies to all of us.

Again, in 2 Timothy 1:7, we see another general original design truth, "*For God has not given us a spirit of fear and timidity, but of power, love, and self-discipline.*" This text, while written to Timothy, was an affirmation by Paul of all of God's children. We can each be affirmed that God designed us to be fearless and filled with power, love, and self-discipline.

What I've described for you here is the process in which we are about to engage: gaining revelation of God's original design, so we have the Designer's objective or "blueprints" in mind. On that note, let's go back to the biblical account of creation—of the first couple—and see what God really had in mind from the very beginning.

■ Back to the Garden

God's original design was for the very first couple—Adam and Eve—to live with joy and unity and fellowship with each other and with God:

Genesis 2:22-25

Then the LORD God made a woman from the rib and brought her to Adam. "At last!" Adam exclaimed. "She is part of my own flesh and bone! She will be called 'woman,' because she was taken out of a man." This explains why a man leaves his father and mother and is joined to his wife, and the two are united into one. Now, although Adam and his wife were both naked, neither of them felt any shame.

I love Adam's response. It's as if he is saying, "This is so cool!" He is clearly excited about what God has done. He is completely jazzed with his new companion.

Do you notice that God's original design for marriage was marked by the absence of self-consciousness? There was only God-consciousness, freedom, unity, perfect relationship, and a complete absence of shame or hiding. How many of us would describe our marriage in those terms? Probably not many.

The mere fact that we may not be experiencing His design at *this* moment does not change or diminish the reality of God's design—or our capacity to get into alignment with it.

There is, however, more to the story. At the very time that God's plan for Kingdom Life and marriage was complete and revealed, an enemy was devising a plan to destroy God's design. Notice the very next words that appear in Scripture following the above passage: *"Now the serpent was the shrewdest of all the creatures the LORD God had made"* (Gen. 3:1). Some would prefer to disregard or downplay the role of Satan in the world. Some would prefer to "just focus on God." That would be a big mistake. To just focus on the devil would be a big mistake, too. But the Scriptures don't ignore Satan. Neither did Jesus (see Mt. 4:10 among dozens of other passages). He is a very real opponent in a very real battle. Dealing with Satan consistent with the way the Bible and Jesus deal with Satan will reflect the truth about God's created economy.

It seems, then, that there was a spiritual battle raging from the earliest of times. As soon as God's original design for humanity and for marriage was unveiled, the Bible tells us that Satan was speaking lies to God's children in an effort to steal from them their Father's original design for their lives and relationships. Satan knew that humanity's alignment with God's design would bring glory to God and power to His children. So he began His strategy to oppose our alignment with it.

Genesis 2:15-17, 3:1-5

The LORD God placed the man in the Garden of Eden to tend and care for it. But the LORD God gave him this warning: "You may freely eat any fruit in the garden except fruit from the tree of the knowledge of good and evil. If you eat of its fruit, you will surely die."

. . . "Really?" he (the serpent) asked the woman. "Did God really say you must not eat any of the fruit in the garden?"

"Of course we may eat it," the woman told him. "It's only the fruit from the tree at the center of the garden that we are not allowed to eat. God says we must not eat it or even touch it, or we will die."

"You won't die!" the serpent hissed. "God knows that your eyes will be opened when you eat it. You will become just like God, knowing everything, both good and evil."

At this point, humanity had the choice to obey God's design and stay in alignment with God's truth, or listen to and obey Satan's lies and rebellion—the same choice we all face many times a day. The rest is history: *"The woman was convinced. The fruit looked so fresh and delicious, and it would make her so wise! So she ate some of the fruit. She also gave some to her husband, who was with her. Then he ate it, too"* (Gen. 3:6).

In that moment everything changed. God's design was compromised by Adam and Eve's choosing. God-consciousness turned to self-consciousness, freedom turned to bondage, unity turned to division, and perfect relationship turned to shame, blame, deception, hiding, and fear:

Genesis 3:7-13

At that moment, their eyes were opened, and they suddenly felt shame at their nakedness. So they strung fig leaves together around their hips to cover themselves. Toward evening they heard the LORD God walking about in the garden, so they hid themselves among the trees. The LORD God called to Adam, "Where are you?"

He replied, "I heard you, so I hid. I was afraid because I was naked."

"Who told you that you were naked?" the LORD God asked. "Have you eaten the fruit I commanded you not to eat?"

"Yes," Adam admitted, "but it was the woman you gave me who brought me the fruit, and I ate it."

Then the LORD God asked the woman, "How could you do such a thing?"

"The serpent tricked me," she replied. "That's why I ate it."

Satan deceived Eve. He lied to her—and she chose to believe the lie. Believing that lie led to sin and disobedience and that disobedience was contagious. In a split second, unity was destroyed, fellowship was shattered, and shame stole Adam and Eve's alignment with God's original design.

Was the problem that Adam and Eve were unable to comply, too young to obey, or too inexperienced to make the right choice? Not at all. It is outside of God's character to create us to obey, expect us to submit, and then not give us the capacity to do so. That would be cruel and unjust—and God is neither of those things. Quite the opposite: God is full love and justice. He seems disappointed when He asks Eve, "*How could you do such a thing*" (verse 13)? Implied in this question is that Adam and Eve had the capacity to obey—even in the face of Satan's lies.

Even when faced with deception, Adam and Eve had the capacity (as do we) for remaining in alignment with God's truth, His design. God's created economy requires alignment with truth. This is true because Kingdom Life as God designed it is centered on truth (Ps. 25:10, 89:14, 111:7; Jn. 4:24; Eph. 5:9). Misalignment comes from believing the lies of Satan and his kingdom. And the biblical word for living out of alignment is *sin*.

Essentially, what happened to Adam and Eve happens to each of us in one way or another. I find, more often than not, that when people are experiencing crisis—or even simply tension—in their marriage, that the source of the crisis or tension can be traced to an area of thinking/behaving that is out of alignment with God's truth.

I have spent a number of years as a marriage and family counselor, pastor, and attorney. I have counseled numerous couples who came to me with their marriages in crisis. They invariably walk into my office or living room complaining about finances, fighting, parenting conflicts, sexual problems, pornography, infidelity, or any other number of tensions. What I always tell them is this: THOSE ARE NOT THE PROBLEM. (That usually gets their attention quickly: "*What do you mean, those aren't the problem?!?*")

Let me repeat myself. Those are not the problem. They are only symptoms of the problem. The real problem is that, down deep, we do not know—and are not living out—God's original design for us. We do not know the Truth about ourselves, or about each other. So we respond to life's hurts and challenges—and to each other—out of human reactions that help us cope and which comfort our fears, pains, and insecurities. Really, the only way to true, lasting transformation is to:

1. expose the untruth at the root of the tension
2. repent of believing and acting out that violation of God's truth and character
3. identify God's truth and original design for the situation
4. intentionally get into alignment (or agreement) with God's truth and design, and live in it

■ God's Design for Our Roles in Marriage

God's design includes the truth about our relationship with Him and with each other. In the Genesis account, we can see that we were designed to live in relationship to our Heavenly Father with God-consciousness, freedom, submission, fellowship, unity, and honesty. And that design isn't limited to how we relate to Him. God's original design also includes the truth about how we were created to live that way in relationship with *each other* in marriage.

I liken this principle to the same truth we can observe on a sports team. I love sports, almost as much as I love cars and motorcycles (and sometimes more!). It's one of my biggest passions in life. And in the course of my lifetime of playing, coaching, and observing many sports teams, I've come to a strong conclusion: teams play better when each player knows his or her position on the court or playing field, is confident in it, has a passion for it, and plays it to the utmost of his or her ability.

On the other hand, when the running back wants to be a quarterback on the football field, or a center tries to play like a guard on the basketball court, confusion ensues and the whole team suffers. Can you imagine what would happen if the goalkeeper suddenly wanted to play forward? Disaster. Ultimately, each of those teams will lose the game and probably have a losing season and short career. That's unfortunate because the individuals on the team are more than likely highly skilled and valuable players—*when they are playing according to their assigned positions.*

Scripture goes on to tell us that God's design for marriage extends to the particular roles that each spouse should fulfill. In a marriage, God's design is for the husband to take the position of leader (1 Cor. 11:3-12; Eph. 5:23). To avoid confusion (because women are certainly designed and gifted for leadership roles, as well), I've come to appreciate the term "gatekeeper" to more succinctly describe a husband's unique and valuable leadership position in marriage.

"Gatekeeper" describes a role that not only is one of *leadership*, but also one of *protection* and *responsibility*, being "on point" for what comes in and out of the household and of the lives of family members. As gatekeepers, we men have a God-given responsibility for such components of our marriage and home life as:

- Spiritual leadership
- Provision
- Protection
- Sacrifice
- Gentleness
- Tenderness
- Initiative
- Wisdom
- Responsibility

God's design for a wife is to complement her husband's leadership by being his helper. There is certainly a huge leadership component in this role, which is why I hesitate to use that term exclusively for the husband. In her capacity as helper and manager, a wife is responsible, among other things, to effectively manage the daily execution of the family's care and activities. Describing a "capable wife," the author of the book of Proverbs writes, *"Her husband has full confidence in her . . . and she watches over the affairs of her household"* (Prov. 31:11, 27 NIV). This portfolio of the wife described in Proverbs 31, if you read the rest of the passage, included running a profitable business, managing a household staff, investing in real estate, extending compassion and charity to the poor, and training her children in wisdom and right living. Now that's a Chief Operations Officer with a pretty impressive job description, if you ask me!

Even more significant is the fact that Scripture calls God Himself a "helper:"

Exodus 18:3-4

Moses said . . . , "My father's God was my helper; he saved me from the sword of Pharaoh."

Deuteronomy 33:29

Blessed are you, O Israel! Who is like you, a people saved by the Lord? He is your shield and helper and your glorious sword.

Psalm 10:14

But you, O God . . . are the helper of the fatherless.

Psalm 27:9

Do not hide your face from me, do not turn your servant away in anger; you have been my helper.

Psalm 118:7

The Lord is with me; he is my helper. I will look in triumph on my enemies.

Hosea 13:9

You are destroyed, O Israel, because you are against me, against your helper.

I believe, from studying these passages, we can confidently assert that accepting the role of "helper" means being one without whom the job doesn't get done. As effective helpers and managers, we can generalize that a wife has a God-given responsibility for such components of marriage and family life as:

- Partnering with her husband in the leadership of the family
- Exercising her strengths to compliment the strengths of her husband
- Creating a peaceful home
- Nurturing the family
- Developing obedient and respectful children
- Prayerful intercession for her family
- Being the "Chief Operations Officer" of the family

Obviously, this is not an exhaustive or even detailed list; I only intend for it to be a sampling of what might be representative of God's design for the respective marriage roles of husbands and wives. My point is not to emphasize the particular "jobs" that go along with those roles. How these roles are actually executed should be determined by each couple together before God. The point is that each person of the marriage team should be comfortable and confident in his or her God-given role—and that together, they honor, respect, and submit to one another within God's established governmental structure. That's the beauty of God's design!

TIME TO DRIVE—Practical Application Exercise for Couples

■ Posture

Buckle up for a lesson in posture. How we posture ourselves as husband and wife before God and each other makes all the difference in the degree to which we experience God's help in creating alignment with His truth. The (physical) posture that best sets us up for alignment, communication, and transformation as we pursue God's design for marriage is one that I call "full engagement and tenderness."

In the following exercise, sit forward facing your spouse, knees to knees. Husbands, take hold of your wife's hands. Look at each other. Some of you have never sat this way in your marriage. Some may find this posture uncomfortable and awkward. Others may find it too confrontational on the one hand or too intimate on the other. That's okay; do it anyway.

It has been amusing to watch couples react when I ask them to do this. One time I was working with a couple and required them to take this posture with each other. Everything was fine until a conflict ensued. Immediately hands were released and both spouses were in the backs of their chairs. That was the posture of disengagement, discouragement, defeat, and defensiveness.

I believe that you will find it very difficult to fight in the posture of full engagement and tenderness. It is important to force yourself, in spite of the awkwardness, to stay in this posture and let the pressure of the posture remind you to remain fully engaged in the process and tender with your spouse.

For those of you who are asking, *"Is this some touchy-feely behavior modification program? Been there, done that, no thanks,"* the answer is, "Absolutely not!" Imagine if a baseball or cricket batter faced away from the pitcher or bowler. What are his chances of a hit? Or what if an Olympic swimmer waited behind the starting blocks until the gun was fired? What would be the chances of a gold medal—or any medal for that matter? Or how about a golfer who looks at the trees as he swings? What are the chances of a solid shot, or even hitting the ball? The answer is slim to none.

In sports, the starting point is always posture—stance, grip, and focus. When someone like a coach or teammate adjusts our stance, grip, or focus, it usually feels awkward at first. But the more we practice, the more comfortable we become. And, if the coaching was good and posture was improved, our performance usually skyrockets.

■ Affirming Your Spouse's Original Design

We should each know the major aspects of our spouse's original design. For example, a wife may be compassionate, joyful, a lover of the outdoors, athletic, bold, and creative. Her husband's original design may be that he was created fearless, strong, a teacher, musical, tenacious, and adventurous.

In the ministry in which Amy and I are involved, we have trained prayer teams who pray with couples and ask the Lord in prayer to reveal the key components of each spouse's original design. If this is available in your own church, I urge you to take advantage of this kind of ministry. But even if you don't, as an initial starting point for this exercise, we will recognize that the major aspects of our original design are somewhat apparent to our spouses.

One question to ask yourself about your spouse's original design is, "What are the tangible positive attributes I believe God created in my spouse?" Another possible question to help uncover each other's original design would be "When my spouse is operating at his or her absolute best, what do I see in him or her that I admire and cherish?"

■ Learning to See and Speak Original Design

Remember Gideon? His original design was not apparent to those around him but God chose to reveal it. This is why we need to learn to pray and hear God's voice through His Spirit so God can reveal truth to us that is not always apparent to our eyes.[2]

Sometimes both the general and personal elements of a person's original design are apparent and sometimes they are not. It is always really powerful and valuable to receive prayer from a trained prayer team where God reveals a person's original design both personally and generally. However, if you and your spouse don't have the opportunity to receive prayer about your original design at this time, you can ask those closest to you what they believe is the truth about who God made you to be, or ask Him yourself in prayer.

For example, if you've noticed that people come to your spouse for advice, that he or she seems to be energized by helping people, and, most importantly, that the help your spouse gives bears godly fruit in people's lives, one component of your spouse's original design may be *wise counselor.* Explaining what you see in terms of specific actions, the life it brings to him or her, and the fruit that results from that action will be particularly helpful in a person understanding and having a revelation of his (or her) original design.

An important ground rule in discerning and speaking original design is that God's design for a person will always be consistent with His truth revealed in Scripture. So, for example, if someone told you that you are a really good liar, you can be assured that those words are not from God. God doesn't make liars and that is clear from Scripture. Therefore, whenever you are considering speaking your observations of someone else's original design, make sure what you are seeing and saying is consistent with Scripture.

Also, we do not want to confuse original design with spiritual gifts. While they may be related and our spiritual gifts may enhance our original design, a key distinction is that original design is who you are and spiritual gifts are given for your work in the body of Christ.

But let's not get too far ahead of ourselves. As a starting point, we can work from observation and begin the process of uncovering our original design.

1. Take a few minutes to consider these questions. Identify and list five to eight of the most prominent aspects of your spouse's original design. If you do not know, ask your spouse what he or she thinks some of those components might be. If your spouse does not know what his or her original design might be, pray with him or her about it, or look into receiving prayer from a prayer team (if this is available to you) for original design.

2. Sit in the posture of full engagement and tenderness. Sit forward knees to knees. Husbands, take both hands of your wife. (Remember, husband, this is your leadership role. Initiate and demonstrate your desire to lead.)

3. Looking your spouse in the eye (husbands go first), affirm the other in who he or she is in the way that God has created him or her. Declare your commitment to help your spouse live in the fullness of how he or she was created by God in his/her original design.

4. In prayer, in front of your partner (husbands go first), thank God for your spouse and declare in prayer whom you believe your spouse to be regarding his/her original design.

CHAPTER TWO

Getting into Alignment

Now turn from your sins and turn to God,
so you can be cleansed of your sins.
Then wonderful times of refreshment will come
from the presence of the Lord . . .

ACTS 3:19-20

Have you ever bought something—say, a bike or a piece of you-assemble-it furniture—and upon reading the directions, been totally overwhelmed by the task at hand? I think of the frustrated parent up until the wee hours of the morning the night before Christmas, holding the directions three different ways, trying to make sense of them. Eventually the poor guy throws the directions out the window and tries to figure it out for himself. When it comes to marriage (and as they say on the popular television commercial), *don't be that guy.*

None of us—not husbands, not wives—have been left on our own to figure out how to get into alignment with God's design. He has given us everything we need in His Word and by His Spirit. We don't need a translator. We just need teachable hearts and a willingness to follow through with the truths we find in His Word, the Scriptures.

■ Jesus Came to Restore God's Design

Jesus came to redeem and restore every way that God's original design was compromised and marred by Satan's intrusion and Adam and Eve's choices. That's an important truth to keep in mind as we're talking about restoring marriages. Jesus came to save, among other things, *your marriage.*

While He was here on earth, Jesus repeatedly stated He had been sent on a mission by God the Father—specifically, a mission to purchase freedom for mankind from the works of the devil (Acts 10:38). In His infinite wisdom and love, God made a provision for us to take back what was lost due to sin and Satan. He sent Jesus to earth to die for our sins, and—in the power of His resurrection—to bring us back into relationship with Him. He wanted not just any relationship with us, but one that would be characterized by "abundance" and "fullness" and "power." A high octane relationship!

Through what we often refer to as "salvation," we receive Jesus' payment for our sins and are saved from the consequences of sin and the power of Satan's kingdom. Ultimately, salvation rescues us from being separated from God in an eternal judgment of darkness and torment. But it also rescues us from the present power of sin in our lives: *"For we know that our old self was crucified with Him so that the body of sin might be done away with, that we should no longer be slaves to sin—because anyone who has died has been freed from sin"* (Rom. 6:6-7, NIV).

The good news of the Gospel doesn't stop there, though. Jesus didn't just come to give us a one-way ticket to heaven when we die. Jesus said He came to seek and save *everything* of God's design that had been compromised or lost.

We know this because of Jesus' statement in Luke 19:10, where He declared He had come to *"seek and save (that which) was lost."* The English word translated "save" in our Bibles in Luke 19:10 is a form of the New Testament word *sozo,* which is a word that includes much more than merely a "spiritual" salvation. In some places in Scripture, the word *sozo* is used to communicate the idea of preserving or rescuing someone from natural dangers and afflictions. It can include saving someone from death or rescuing someone out of mortal danger. Based on its use and context elsewhere in Scripture, it also means saving someone from disease and delivering him into good health, or setting someone free from demonic affliction. It communicates bringing someone to a point of thriving. It also is used in the spiritual sense of saving someone from eternal death to eternal life in relationship with God.[3]

A form of the word *sozo* is used over 100 times in the New Testament translated with such English words as "cured," "get well," "made well," "recover," "restore," "save," and "saved." In each case, *sozo* marks a moment when God's power intersects with the lives of people and amazing stuff happens. Following are a few ways the word *sozo* is used to demonstrate the broad spectrum of God's power released for salvation or restoration:[4]

Romans 10:9-10 NIV

If you confess with your mouth, "Jesus is Lord," and believe in your heart that God raised him from the dead, you will be saved. For it is with your heart that you believe and are justified, and it is with your mouth that you confess and are saved (sozo, emphasis added).

Sozo also is used in Scripture to communicate a healing or restoration of the inner person. The inner person is generally referred to as one's "soul," which is comprised of our mind, emotions, and will. This is where we live under siege by the enemy's lies and torments, sorrows and heartaches, inferiorities and inadequacies, arrogances and strivings, and more. One of many accounts of Jesus' ministry found in the Gospels speaks to this reality:

Luke 8:35-36 NIV

The people went out to see what had happened. When they came to Jesus, they found the man from whom the demons had gone out, sitting at Jesus' feet, dressed and in his right mind; and they were afraid. Those who had seen it told the people how the demon-possessed man had been cured *(sozo, emphasis added).*

Another dimension in which the word *sozo* is used is in reference to physical healings. The salvation and restoration piece of Jesus' mission to restore us to God's original design included physical healings. The Gospel of Mark describes Jesus healing a blind man so he regained sight and was made well:

Mark 10:52 NIV

"Go," said Jesus, "your faith has healed *(sozo) you. Immediately he received his sight and followed Jesus along the road" (emphasis added).*

We could continue with many biblical examples of Jesus' *sozo* work, but the bottom line is that when Jesus came to save what was lost it involved much more than merely getting people into heaven. That certainly is foundational but it does not stop there—it merely begins at that point. As good as that is, it is just the beginning of the good news. Jesus' redemptive work began with restoring the relationship between God and man through a spiritual salvation, but even our spiritual salvation will affect our thinking, emotions, choices, activities, and—very importantly, our *marriages.*

■ Alignment with God's Original Design

So how, exactly, do you get a marriage into alignment with God's original design? What does *sozo* (healing, wholeness, restoration, etc.) look like for a marriage relationship? How do you unwind the years of habits and patterns, hurts and fears that have paralyzed your capacity to change, and then move forward in wholeness and health? How do you create and maintain a new marriage that experiences the power of God's design? It's simple—but not easy.

I've given you a bit of a Bible lesson in these first two chapters because that's where we must go to find our answer. That's certainly where Amy and I found our answer—and so have countless other couples with whom we've worked.

There is a plethora of marriage books, courses, and counselors out there that can give you a lot of information about behavior modification, emotional healing, and all kinds of innovations in counseling. I know—I have spent a number of years as a marriage and family counselor utilizing those tools (and those aren't all bad). Many of them contain some really great stuff. But bottom line, I have found that many of those programs have limited effectiveness because they don't start and end with God's original design or God's power to move into alignment with His design.

I've found it is only when a couple is desperate for transformation in their marriage, when both partners are committed to bringing that marriage back into alignment with God's design, and when they are willing to follow the biblical directions for getting there that they invariably reach their destination.

Are you in?

If so, let's start by getting a clear understanding of how we appropriate Jesus' life-giving *(sozo)* power. Then let's apply His life-giving power to our marriages to get us back into perfect alignment with God's design.

■ The Quickest Route to Alignment

You may be surprised to know that the quickest route to alignment with God's original design is *repentance*. Many of the people with whom Amy and I counsel and pray regarding their marriages look at us dumbfounded when we tell them that. Generally they are each looking at each other's faults and flaws as the culprit in the marriage, not their own. Isn't that the way most of us think?

The Scriptures are clear, however, that we each need to look at ourselves first. The Bible is also clear that *repentance and forgiveness* are the way we appropriate the work of Jesus on the cross and apply His healing power to our lives. Repentance is the way we have access to the transforming power of God, the transforming power of forgiveness, and the transforming power of Life. In this light, repentance takes on a whole new connotation. Rather than being a guilt-ridden, embarrassing religious obligation, repentance becomes a joyful gift that we can embrace as the full extension of God's mercy.

Repentance is also the primary tool that brings transformation. It opens the door to His ultimate "power to change." It postures us for forgiveness, which is what cancels our debt of sin. It makes a way for a restored relationship with our Heavenly Father and with the people around us (including our spouse). Deeply situated in God's truth of forgiveness is the very power of Life, the only power that brings real and permanent transformation to a marriage or to anything else.

Repentance is the only way we can experience God's transforming power in our lives.

I believe the emphasis on repentance is what sets this book apart from most others on the marriage-and-family-shelf at your local bookstore. It is through authentic repentance and forgiveness that we appropriate Jesus' redemptive work on the cross. It is through authentic repentance and forgiveness that God transforms us. And it is through authentic repentance and forgiveness that God transforms our marriages.

Jim and Megan are a great example of the power of repentance and forgiveness to transform a marriage. Both came into marriage out of lives of brokenness and abuse, from families of origin that had been through multiple marriages and divorces. As a result, Megan was living in a self-imposed world of rules, boundaries, and walls. She thought by controlling everything around her it would give her security, including setting rules for Jim.

Jim's coping mechanism, on the other hand, was to avoid conflict like the plague and compliantly follow the rules Megan set. On the inside, however, he was disconnected from his wife emotionally, physically, and spiritually—leaving Megan feeling like he was not interested in her or invested in the marriage.

That's when Megan received what she described as a vision from the Lord. It was similar to a slow motion movie clip of what life was like for Jim, trying to be her husband. She describes it being "as easy as loving a porcupine." Her heart broke. The Holy Spirit began to show her where pride and arrogance and the need to always be right made it impossible for Jim to lead and protect. The revelation that she had been far from the wife God had designed her to be landed on her heart like a ton of bricks.

Megan showed up on our doorstep completely broken and desperate. She was willing to do anything to salvage her marriage. Was it too late, she wondered?

Amy and I shot straight with both her and Jim: If their marriage was going to survive and thrive, they both needed a change of heart and a dedicated commitment to the process. They agreed. First assignment: We had them hold hands, look at each other, and begin the process of each identifying personal sins and failings—no finger pointing. This healing process went on for several months: holding hands every night and confessing, repenting before the Lord together and asking forgiveness, praying with and for each other, and speaking words of blessing into one another's lives. In fact, one of their assignments at the beginning was that they could ONLY speak words of blessing in their home. They had to train themselves and their children in learning to speak only blessing and words of life in their home. Needless to say, it was pretty quiet for a few days until the concept caught on.

Out of their mutual repentance and forgiveness, Jim and Megan created healthy boundaries to protect their marriage and put into place actions that would begin to rebuild trust. Megan let go of the stranglehold she had placed on her marriage and began to trust God and her husband to lead her. Jim re-engaged as the gatekeeper of his wife and family.

Six months after our first meeting, Jim and Megan were a completely transformed couple. Jim was joy-filled, confident, leading his family, and completely adoring Megan. Megan, who had never known till now what peace and protection felt like, was a new woman who radiated gentleness and peace. Today, we see Jim and Megan on a regular basis. Their lives and marriage give testimony to the fact that God honors repentance. In fact, there has been such a transformation that when Jim ran into an old friend, his friend recognized the change and asked what was different. Within three weeks he and his wife were sitting down with us to experience the same kind of restoration and healing!

■ How Can We Get Some of That?

Repentance may seem like a foreign or old-fashioned concept to you, but it's really very simple. True repentance is composed of two parts: confession and obedience. Each of these is distinct and essential to the release of the power of the cross into our lives and marriages. Typically, most of us have understood repentance to be synonymous with confession. But the richness of the original

Greek word actually emphasizes *obedience*. The word Jesus uses, which we translate "repent," means a complete turn around or 180-degree turn. It emphasizes *action*, not just confession. "Confession" refers to the words we use and "obedience" refers to the actions we take consistent with those words; the power of the cross is accessed through both. Confession alone falls short of the biblical truth of repentance. It lacks the transformational power intended by God to bring restoration.

Repentance is more than saying "I'm sorry."

Transformational confession demands that we accurately identify, acknowledge, and express our sin and take responsibility for it. This is true both horizontally and vertically. When we ask for forgiveness from our spouse it is important to clearly confess and acknowledge our sin. The same is true with God. There is power in our spoken words and there is spiritual significance in accurately and authentically confessing specific sin.

Another important element of biblical confession is the need to be thorough. When you recognize that the enemy is a roaring lion crouching at the door looking for someone to devour (1 Pet. 5:8), your sensitivity is heightened. You want to avoid having any residual or unconfessed sin that would provide access for the enemy.

One of the first areas of repentance for Amy and me included confessing and turning from the various ways we had been living in fear. At the beginning of chapter one I talked about why fear is not part of our original design. Let's go back to that issue and use it as an example (although you can certainly apply this principle to whatever issue you and your spouse are dealing with). What is really important is that withholding any part of our sin will compromise any true alignment. If John and Megan had withheld parts of their sin, they would not have experienced true alignment and the new life that comes with it. An example of *thorough* confession of the sin of fear might look as follows:

To my spouse:

"I have believed the lie of fear and I have been operating in it. I know that fear is not from God; it is from the enemy. I have not trusted you. I have not believed God's Word that says, 'Do not fear.' I have not taken a stand on faith and love which overcomes all fear. It is my sin and I take full responsibility for it. I am sorry for the way that my fear has diminished you and allowed disunity, insecurity, and anxiety into our marriage. Will you forgive me for my sin of fear and all of the ways it has affected our marriage?"

The importance of saying the words, "Will you forgive me" cannot be overemphasized. This is equally true for the words, "I forgive you." It is also important, critical really, that we share our heart of remorse for ways our sin has hurt our spouse and others. Although saying "I'm sorry" isn't enough to bring a spiritual transaction, it is absolutely necessary for healing and reconnecting. So be sure in your repentance with each other that you are thorough in expressing your recognition of the hurt you have caused, and your remorse for causing it.

To the Lord:

"Father, please forgive me for believing the lie of fear. It is not from You and it is not my design. I confess every form of fear that I have allowed to rule my mind. I have been afraid that You would not come through. I have been afraid that I am alone. I have been afraid that there is no hope. I have been afraid of what will happen to me. This fear is not in alignment with Your truth. I ask Your forgiveness for my sin of fear."

Once thorough confession has been done, the second part of repentance kicks in—obedience. Obedience is the highest expression of our love for God. In the case of John and Megan, John actually changed careers in response to what God revealed it would take to put his wife and family first and get into alignment with God's truth in his life.

John 14:15, 21

If you love me, you will obey what I command . . . Whoever has my commands and obeys them, he is the one who loves me. He who loves me will be loved by my Father, and I too will love him and show myself to him.

Obedience is also behavioral alignment with God's truth. It is establishing integrity between what we say (confession) and what we do (obedience). It is this integrity and consistency that make repentance effective and powerful. In repentance, we turn from our sin and run into intimacy, obedience, and alignment with God. This is where spiritual acceleration happens, where we crank up the throttle on transformation. Why? Because of the necessity of humility. It takes radical humility to repent authentically. And God cannot resist a humble heart.

■ The Power of Immediate Forgiveness

The decision to forgive is the highest octane fuel that can be found on the planet. It is forgiveness that releases the power of God to conquer death and restore life to God's children. Forgiveness is the whole ball game. Immediately on the heels of repentance comes the need to both grant and receive forgiveness. Receiving God's forgiveness is a critical tool for transformation, as is granting and receiving forgiveness from one another.

So often I hear couples express a fear of repentance because they are certain they will not be forgiven, that they could not be forgiven. Yet in working with marriages over the past twenty years, I have never seen a spouse refuse to forgive the most grievous of sins when approached with *authentic* repentance. In fact, those dramatic encounters are more often than not the most profound and holy moments of radical transformation and healing that pave the way for alignment and restoration.

■ Receiving Forgiveness

Receiving forgiveness—whether from God or from a spouse—can be more difficult than it sounds. We think we want forgiveness and wonder why we would resist such a gift of freedom. Yet, when we are faced with the weight of our sin and our (perceived) unworthiness of forgiveness, we can sometimes fail to allow forgiveness a home in our heart. We may repent but still hold on to the burden of sin and thereby nullify the work of Jesus Christ in His sacrifice on the cross. We fail to believe that He went to the cross willingly and out of love for us. We fail to accept that His power does erase our sin at the moment of genuine repentance.

What I've just described for you here is *shame.* Shame is not from God. Believing and living in the lie of shame often paralyzes individuals from experiencing the freedom created by forgiveness. But in the moment forgiveness is received, the chains of shame are snapped and God's love and healing begin to pour in.

■ Granting Forgiveness

Equally important is God's mandate to extend to others the forgiveness He has given us—not only once, and not only when they repent or ask for forgiveness. God commands to forgive all offenses against us *immediately* and *unconditionally*.

Colossians 3:13

You must make allowance for each other's faults and forgive the person who offends you. Remember, the Lord forgave you, so you must forgive others.

We are commanded and empowered to forgive regardless of whether the offender has asked for forgiveness

---

This sounds challenging and indeed, certainly feels challenging (or perhaps impossible and offensive) in the wake of a serious offense or a long history of marital disappointment or abuse. Like so many things in God's design, it is counter-intuitive. And yet, the person who is willing to obey and forgive immediately and without condition will experience true transformation and freedom from the poison of bitterness, resentment, and unforgiveness. That kind of obedience, that kind of forgiveness, sets off a chain of events in the heavenly realms that opens the floodgates of heaven for supernatural healing and restoration — like nothing else!

This was the experience of our friend, Samantha, who was the classic "all-American mom." She was married and had three wonderful children. They lived in a big home in a beautiful neighborhood. She was fortunate to be a stay-at-home mom. Her warmth and gift for compassion drew others to her. And to top it off, she was beautiful, tender, and funny.

Samantha grew up in a church where the only things she remembered repeating were the same prayers over and over. One prayer in particular went like this: *"Forgive us our trespasses as we forgive those who trespass against us."* She grew up believing that God was distant, un-reachable, non-communicative, and demanding of payment for her sin. It wasn't until she experienced the most painful situation in her life that she came to understand just how close, real, loving, and forgiving God is.

Without any warning, her husband Jerry came home from work one day and quickly moved out. The pain was so great even breathing became a challenge. The flood of emotions never seemed to let up and she plummeted into a deep depression. Her joy and energy were stripped away along with the ability to give any attention to her children. They all coped by retreating to their own places in their big house and quietly suffering alone.

As time went on, Jerry's deception of financial mismanagement and infidelity surfaced. He had been covering up for years with lies. The more Samantha learned, the angrier she became. She became enraged and then paralyzed by feelings of rejection, abandonment, and fear. She became tormented by her own thoughts and imagination and an ugly bitterness and resentment grew inside her. The roots took hold and insidiously claimed every part of her life.

Eventually, Samantha didn't care about anything except "pay back," and a desire to hurt Jerry as much as he had hurt her. She slandered him, telling her story over and over wherever she could find a listening ear. Unwilling to move forward, she stayed in the past, revisiting it over and over. Eventually her children followed her down that path and their home became one of sorrow, despair, anger, hopelessness, disorder, chaos, and isolation.

Then friends invited Samantha to a new church. There she was surrounded by people who poured out more love on her than she knew what to do with. It gave her a glimpse of what joy, peace, and hope looked like in the lives of real people who embraced repentance and forgiveness as a way of life. She wanted to see more of that, so kept attending. As she did, she was faced with the truth that she is called to forgive—everyone, every time, even Jerry. Samantha broke. She repented of her unforgiveness. She fully released Jerry of everything; he had no debt to pay. She gave up her right to "understand" why his rejection and abandonment had happened. She replaced bondage, resentment, and bitterness with forgiveness and freedom.

Samantha now says this, "God makes good on His promises. My life has been redeemed and restored and blessed beyond what I imagined. I feel His love, protection, provision, peace, strength, and joy—every day. As difficult as it was to offer unconditional forgiveness, I know now it is ABSOLUTELY the only way."

Samantha has since remarried and has a joyful, healthy relationship with her new husband. Because she forgave, she was able to enter her new marriage free from any lingering baggage from the old. By her own admission, repentance and forgiveness made all the difference in the world.

Note that Jesus did not encourage us to forgive; He *commanded* it. That makes unforgiveness a sin, which gives a mighty foothold to the enemy who will use it to harden our hearts and break up our marriages. Bitterness, the Bible tells us, causes us to miss the grace of God and defiles everyone and everything around us (Heb. 12:15). Anger and unforgiveness give a place—*topos*—to the devil in our lives (Eph. 4:26-27). That Greek word *topos*, used in the original writing of the New Testament Scriptures, is interesting. It means a tangible place or spot in our lives. Hanging onto unforgiveness literally opens the door to the devil in our marriages. Overcoming unforgiveness is absolutely central to the restoration of God's design for marriage.[5]

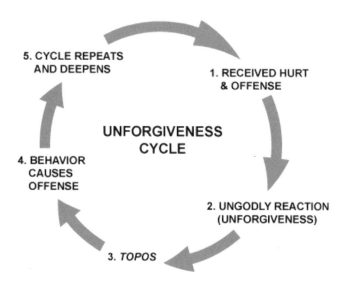

We all have the capacity to forgive any offense. The refusal to forgive will be worse than the hurt of the offense itself because refusal to forgive is permanent imprisonment to the offense and the offender. The decision to forgive—whether I feel like it or not, whether the offender has demonstrated remorse or not, whether the person has apologized or not—will break the chains of unforgiveness and offense and open the floodgates of freedom and life and healing. That's real power.

The decision to forgive—whether I feel like it or not, whether the offender has demonstrated remorse or not, whether the person has apologized or not—will break the chains of unforgiveness and offense and open the floodgates of freedom and life and healing.

Amy and I witnessed this in our work with a young couple named Kevin and Christina. They were carrying years of anger and wounding, which was choking the life right out of them. To make matters worse, in their church group they were witnessing marriages all around them becoming stronger and operating in greater unity than they had ever witnessed before. They, however, continued sliding downward into the terrible pit of unforgiveness.

What was revealed when we met with them was a pattern of intimidation, anger, control, hopelessness, and victimization. At first, both claimed they were willing to do whatever it took to make the marriage work. They went through an intensive process of asking and granting forgiveness for past sins and hurt. Unfortunately, they went through the motions without truly granting forgiveness. Confessions were used as fresh ammunition to wound each other. They became less and less engaged in their commitment to follow through with assignments. It became apparent that we wanted restoration for them more than they wanted it for themselves.

We knew God's design was for Kevin and Christina to be a dynamite couple with a high octane relationship with Him and each other. But their disobedience to God's truth and commands to live out of a heart of forgiveness and kindness kept them locked down in destructive patterns like the unforgiveness cycle illustrated on the previous page. Their passivity and victimization paralyzed the healing God wanted for their marriage. They wanted the "good fruit" they saw others producing but were not willing to go through the pruning process.

It does not matter how great a mentor or counselor a couple has working with them. No other person can offer repentance and forgiveness for another marriage and expect that marriage to be changed. We each have to take responsibility for ourselves and obediently align ourselves to God's truth for marriage. If Amy and I could have had this couple learn one truth it would have been this: the power of the cross is powerful enough to crush anything that raises its ugly head against God's design for their marriage. Apply the cross through 100% confession, repentance, and extending and receiving forgiveness and you will begin to live in a whole new realm that is far better than anything or anyone can humanly dream up. I'm sad to say, Kevin and Christina were unwilling to embrace that truth. The results were tragic — and they didn't need to be.

In God's economy, there is no real choice. It's a decision between life and death, bondage or freedom, hurt or healing. I have seen couples forgive each other for the most grievous of offenses and find a new life, a new marriage, and complete healing. I have also seen couples refuse to forgive for much less grievous offenses and remain stuck in their imprisonment and locked down in their marriage.

■ A Prescription for Transformation — The 4Rs

A helpful model Amy and I use to appropriate God's gifts of repentance and forgiveness — and to get us back into alignment with God's design for us as individuals and as a marriage team — is what we commonly refer to as the "4R's." This was the model John and Megan used as they worked through the repentance and forgiveness process with God and with each other, as did Samantha. It's a model I hope you, too, will learn to use freely and regularly.

This transactional prayer model, introduced in the *Living Free Course*[6], is a great spiritual tool that simply outlines the biblical prescription for confession, repentance, exercising authority in Christ, and receiving God's forgiveness and the power of His Spirit to move in the opposite direction of a sin or untruth. Basically the 4R's include:

1. **Repent & Receive** (**Repent** and **receive** the Lord's forgiveness)

Humbly submit yourself before God in repentance for your sin—for any actions, attitudes, or neglect that violate His Word, character, love, or truth—and receive His forgiveness through Christ's death and resurrection. This can include granting and asking for forgiveness.

Acts 3:19-20

Repent, then, and turn to God, so that your sins may be wiped out, that times of refreshing may come from the Lord.

2. **Rebuke & Renounce** (**Rebuke** every influence the enemy has used to energize this sin in your life and marriage and **renounce** the lies that contradict God's truth)

Resist the enemy and any tormenting spirits by rebuking them through the authority and power of the death and resurrection of Jesus Christ. In God's authority, renounce any lies believed about yourself, God, or others.

Matthew 4:10

Jesus said to him, "Away from me, Satan! For it is written: 'Worship the Lord your God, and serve him only.'"

Luke 10:17, 19-20

And the seventy returned with joy, saying, "Lord, even the demons are subject to us in Your name." . . . "I have given you authority to trample on snakes and scorpions and to overcome all the power of the enemy; nothing will harm you. However, do not rejoice that the spirits submit to you, but rejoice that your names are written in heaven."

3. **Replace & Renew** (**Confess** your commitment to walk in the truth and renew your mind in the truth. Name specific ways you will do this.)

Come near to God through washing your hands of sinful behavior and attitudes, and cleansing your mind of duplicity in your devotion to God. Replace it with obedience and with a single-focused devotion to God. Ask God to renew your heart, mind, emotions, and will through the empowering of the Holy Spirit.

Ephesians 4:22-24

You were taught, with regard to your former way of life, to put off your old self, which is being corrupted by its deceitful desires; to be made new in the attitude of your minds; and to put on the new self, created to be like God in true righteousness and holiness.

4. **Receive & Rejoice** (**Receive** the infilling work of God's Spirit)

Claim, and receive in faith, the empowering/infilling work of the Holy Spirit to walk in His ways. Rejoice in the abundant grace and peace that is yours in the Holy Spirit!

Titus 3:4-6

But when the kindness and love of God our Savior appeared, He saved us, not because of righteous things we had done, but because of His mercy. He saved us through the washing of rebirth and renewal by the Holy Spirit, whom He poured out on us generously through Jesus Christ our Savior.

■ An Example of a 4R Prayer

The 4R-prayer model is simply that—a model. Not a formula. Not a pre-scription. Some have found it helpful to hear what it sounds like to repent, rebuke, replace, and receive. Below is just a sample of what a 4R-prayer might sound like. Yours will be different—because you are *you*. And you don't need to make yours sound exactly like this one. You just need to make sure you cover each point thoroughly between you and God: *repent* (of your sin; call it what it is), *rebuke* (any way the enemy has gained access to your life in and through that sin), *replace* (the sin or wrong thinking with right actions and the truth), and *receive* (God's forgiveness and the power of His Holy Spirit).

Just for an example, here is what John, in the story about John and Megan above, may have prayed as he and Megan were contending for restoration and alignment in their marriage:

Repent and receive:
Father, forgive me for failing to lead my family, for being disengaged and pas-sive in leading and loving my wife. Forgive me for being self-absorbed and full of entitlements to meet my own needs and forgetting my role in this family. These are my sins and I take full responsibility for them. They are forms of pride and rebel-lion. I have sinned against You and against Your truth in my life. I confess every form of selfishness and distraction. I confess the idolatry of self and self-interest. Please forgive me. Wash me clean, Lord. Take my sin from me as far as the East is from the West.

Father, I receive Your forgiveness through the cross of Jesus Christ. I receive the truth that I stand forgiven not because of anything I have done, but all because of what Jesus has done for me. Thank You for the cross!

Rebuke and renounce:

As a forgiven child of God, I stand in Jesus' Name and declare that I renounce passivity in all its forms. I renounce the deception that comes from living in sin. I renounce operating in rebellion and pride and I rebuke and resist all influence of the enemy in my life through these sins. I break their hold on my life and sever the chains that have held me down. I will not be imprisoned by their lies or deception any longer. I command them to be gone in Jesus' Name!

Replace and renew:

I replace my sin with the truth that I am the bold, fearless, and fully committed leader of my family. I am fully equipped by God's design to lead my wife in our life together. I replace passivity, pride, and rebellion with active humility and obedience. I replace self with Christ as the center and Lord of my life, and I renew my thinking in alignment with His truth and character.

Receive—and rejoice!

Father, fill me up with your Holy Spirit. Set me free to run in my original design. Make me want to obey You and Your truth, and fill me with Your power to do so. Impart to me humility and strength. Make me more like Your Son, Jesus. Let my joy overflow as I run into alignment with His truth!

When we pray this way, we experience a "spiritual transaction." A spiritual transaction is an interaction with God in which we do our part and He does His. When we pray prayers of salvation, repentance, and forgiveness—to name a few—we engage in the wonderful, grace-filled interaction of the "human-divine cooperative." That means when we do, as human beings, what we are required biblically to do, God moves in and responds with what only He can do—that is, release His power into our lives to effect the transformation that only He can bring.

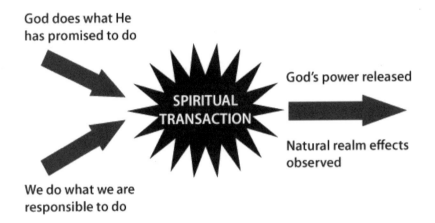

I know I want that for my marriage—don't you? Bottom line, spiritual transaction is simply **the power of God actually transforming our life and marriage.** Without it we're sunk. It's not some weird humming or dancing around. It's repentance; it's forgiveness; it's humility; it's hunger for more. I am here to say it is real. It is not religion. It is power.

God's power, and only God's power, changed my life—and my marriage. I needed spiritual transaction—not techniques, not theories, and not a list of do's and don'ts. I needed the power of God, which is available by His Holy Spirit to all who will repent and obey Him.

Every chapter in this book is about getting to spiritual transaction. Getting to God's power experienced in your life. Real freedom from sin. Real freedom from hurts. Real freedom from injustices and abuse. Real healing in your marriage. Real unity. Real life!

TIME TO DRIVE—Practical Application Exercise for Couples

■ Practicing Repentance and Forgiveness

When I first got my motorcycle I didn't have a license. I had to go to a class to learn "how to ride safely." Of course, I had ridden motorcycles since I was a kid. I went into the class thinking, "This is a bit ridiculous." But given that it was required, I played along. You guessed it: I was shocked at what I didn't know—even from an entry level class! The point: Just because we are starting out slow, don't "cop an attitude" about the assignments. Follow them precisely. Don't shortcut or change the assignment or the rules. And DON'T, under any circumstances, enter into the assignments half-heartedly. That will be a waste of time. (Have I mentioned that I hate to waste time?)

1. Each of you, take out some notepaper and a pen. Start a list of the things for which you would like to ask your husband's or wife's forgiveness. (If you can't think of anything, ask the Lord to show you. Ultimately, if you believe you are completely innocent, you should throw this book in the trash. Either you don't need it or it can't help you!) List the areas where you know there are hurts, dysfunctional patterns, unforgiveness, or anything else that stands between you and your honey.

2. Sit in the posture of full engagement and tenderness. Sit forward knees to knees with the husband taking both hands of the wife. Husband, this is your leadership role to initiate and demonstrate your desire to lead.

3. Husbands go first. Take the first thing on your list and repent authentically and thoroughly, asking your wife for forgiveness.

    Here is one of mine you can use as a sample: *Sweetie, I have not been leading us in praying together everyday. It is my responsibility and I have completely failed. I know how important praying together is for us, and especially how important it is to you and for you to feel connected and protected. I am so sorry I have hurt you by this. I have no excuse. I take full responsibility for this. It is a form of passivity which is rebellion. God designed me to lead and I fully intend to lead us in prayer together everyday. Will you please forgive me?*

4. Wives make this decision and declaration immediately and out loud: *I forgive you.*

5. Next, wives, repent of your first item. Husbands, respond with forgiveness: *I forgive you.*

6. Take turns working through your lists. Don't worry if this takes several sessions. Be thorough.

Please remember this is only the start. Each of you must follow through with obedience to the commitments that you made in order for transactional change to take place. Otherwise, this was just a religious exercise—and we don't want anything to do with that.

CHAPTER THREE

The Non-Negotiables

So humble yourselves before God. Resist the devil,
and he will flee from you.
Draw close to God, and God will draw close to you.
Wash your hands, you sinners; purify your hearts, you hypocrites.
Let there be tears for the wrong things you have done . . .
When you bow down before the Lord and admit
your dependence on him,
he will lift you up and give you honor.

JAMES 4:7-10

Frank and Stacy sat down, swallowed hard, and simply said, "We need help with our marriage." They confessed they were desperate and had nowhere else to turn. They were at their wits' end and, if something didn't change soon, the marriage would be over. Frank and Stacy then proceeded to describe years of hurt and anger, distrust and abuse—a long and painful list. They claimed they agreed on one thing, though: they were willing to do whatever it would take to rebuild their marriage.

We all started out hopeful. As they were given assignments, however, Frank and Stacy would go through the motions but could never get past their past. Their history of hurt held too strong a grip on them and the efforts to address patterns and opposition to their marriage became toxic and destructive. Neither husband nor wife was able to trust the power of God's truth to bring healing to the past. They both *said* they wanted things to be different. But fundamentally Frank and Stacy didn't really agree about actually doing what it would take for them to experience real transformation. Consequently, little progress was made over several years of effort.

■ The Need for Desperation

It's one thing to feel desperate and say we are desperate. It's another thing entirely to be willing to ask for forgiveness, admit wrongs and mistakes, and grant forgiveness for past hurts. That is authentic desperation, and authentic desperation is the heart condition that leads to transformation. In our experience, every couple that has been willing to ask for and grant genuine forgiveness, and allow God to bring them into alignment with His truth, has experienced His life-giving power and transformation in their life and marriage. Conversely, every couple that has been unwilling to do so has not.

Kevin and Shannon's story turned out much differently than Frank and Stacy's. When they first met with us, the only thing they could agree on was that they could not go on. They didn't want to go on, not if things didn't change dramatically. But essentially there was no hope for change. Neither one had the energy to make change happen. Neither had the energy to deal with the years of stockpiled pain and anger. They were locked down and defeated. Hopeless and despairing. The only thing holding the marriage together was the absence of energy to end it.

They decided to make a last-ditch effort to call for help—which was where Amy and I came in. In that moment, each was confronted with this question, "Are you willing to do whatever it takes to put this marriage back together?"

It was important for Amy and me to tell this couple that they did not need to know "how" to fix their marriage. They didn't need to know the way out. But they did need to be willing to do whatever was asked by those who do.

Kevin and Shannon did say "yes" to that important question—and proceeded to re-write everything about their marriage over the next several months. They repented, they forgave, they exercised authority, and they effectively dismantled the destructive spiritual roots and patterns attacking their marriage. That was the tangible evidence of their genuine desperation. As of the writing of this page, two years later, their marriage is completely restored and they are ministering to other couples in crisis. God completely honored their genuine desperation and hunger for a marriage in alignment with His design.

Desperation: the willingness to do whatever it takes to get there.

This is the true measure of desperation. True desperation will not give up or give in when the process becomes difficult or seemingly unbearable. True desperation won't compromise when its expectations aren't being met and its timeline isn't working out. True desperation is an essential component of a transformed marriage.

■ Living in Biblical Unity

There are several truths revealed in Genesis 2 that make up the framework for alignment to God's original design for marriage, but one truth is at the heart of all the others—unity. Recently, the word "unity" has become soft. By that I mean that "unity" these days can refer to just about anything. The word has lost its edge and consequently its power. "Unity" today often means "tolerance for the lowest common ground to avoid conflict." On the outside that looks like peace. But on the inside that recipe for unity will suck the life out of you. Tolerance is not the answer to the world's problems—truth is.

Tolerance is not the answer to the world's problems—truth is.

The truth about unity lies in its two core meanings: "oneness" and "agreement."[7] In the biblical understanding of unity, there is oneness between us and God and oneness between each other. It is vertical and horizontal. There is agreement between us about God's truth, that alignment with God's truth is the only way to experience LIFE. Oneness is developed by agreement. Agreement is the practical step that, over time, in the face of opposition and through every storm, builds oneness.

Genesis 2:23-25

"At last!" Adam exclaimed. "She is part of my own flesh and bone! She will be called 'woman,' because she was taken out of a man." This explains why a man leaves his father and mother and is joined to his wife, and the two are united into one.

Unity (or agreement) is both conceptual *and* behavioral. We can't just *say* we agree. We must also demonstrate agreement by our worldview and our conduct. The level of commitment that we bring to agreement is everything. The unapologetic and relentless defense of real agreement is necessary.

True unity means having NOTHING "in between us"—no anger, exasperation, frustration, blame, or record-keeping. When I am functioning in unity with others (and with my wife, specifically), it means being more "for the team" than for myself. To draw on a sports analogy, it means submitting myself to the Rulebook, and to an Umpire other than my own feelings or entitlements. Building the biblical stronghold of unity requires complete agreement on the rules for a great marriage—and then both partners playing by those rules.

■ The Non-Negotiables for Building a High Octane Marriage

"Rules? I hate rules. Who are you to impose rules on me? Rules are for kindergarteners. Adults have graduated far beyond the need for rules. But, if we must have rules, let's at least call them 'kind suggestions' or 'guidelines.' Let's at least give adults the credit to use their discretion about which rules to obey and when to obey them."

That was me. From the time I was 12, I was bucking the system of authority. And I know I'm not alone. Ever since the modern rebellion against authority which found its pinnacle in the 1960s, the concept of rules has become unpopular in Western culture. We have been fed the lie that rules are constraining and life-sucking. That is a lie from the enemy—the devil—who knows the clarity of rules bring will allow for agreement and unity to be established. Where unity is established in marriages and families, God's power can be released. No wonder the enemy hates rules!

We have discovered that some key "rules of the road" for a high octane marriage are **mutual brokenness, mutual submission, and mutual engagement:**

- *Mutual brokenness* is the absence of self-centeredness and pride.
- *Mutual submission* is the absence of fear and control.
- *Mutual engagement* is the absence of passivity.

On the other hand:

- *Self-centeredness and pride* are the opposite of brokenness.
- *Control and fear* are the opposite of submission.
- *Passivity* is the opposite of engagement.

■ Mutual Brokenness

A popular use of the word "brokenness" is to describe those who are hurt, wounded, or victimized. I am using the word as it is used in Scripture and in a much more positive sense. Biblical brokenness reflects a heart condition of (and a choice for) submission and God-centeredness, rather than one of pride, self-focus, and staying mired in one's circumstances. Brokenness is an indicator of humility—and humility has a spiritual fragrance that attracts God's favor. Jesus is the perfect example of biblical brokenness:

Philippians 2:3-11 NIV

Do nothing out of selfish ambition or vain conceit, but in humility consider others better than yourselves. Each of you should look not only to your own interests, but also to the interests of others. Your attitude should be the same as that of Christ Jesus: Who, being in very nature God, did not consider equality with God something to be grasped, but made himself nothing, taking the very nature of a servant, being made in human likeness. And being found in appearance as a man, he humbled himself and became obedient to death—even death on a cross! Therefore God exalted him to the highest place and gave him the name that is above every name, that at the name of Jesus every knee should bow, in heaven and on earth and under the earth, and every tongue confess that Jesus Christ is Lord, to the glory of God the Father.

Biblical brokenness is also illustrated many times in God's relationship with the community of faith in the Old Testament. In Exodus 32:9, God referred to the Israelites as a "stiff-necked people." But He constantly assured them that if they would break their stiff-necked rebellion and humble themselves with a contrite heart, He would bless them. In my experience, this is always true. Brokenness is the antidote for pride and a surefire way to attract God's blessing and favor.

Psalm 51:16-17 NIV

You do not delight in sacrifice, or I would bring it; you do not take pleasure in burnt offerings. The sacrifices of God are a broken spirit; a broken and contrite heart, O God, you will not despise.

2 Chronicles 7:14 NIV

If my people, who are called by my name, will humble themselves and pray and seek my face and turn from their wicked ways, then will I hear from heaven and will forgive their sin and will heal their land.

Brokenness is asking the question at every turn,

"Lord, what are you showing me, ABOUT ME?"

That's what true humility sounds like.

True brokenness simply recognizes that I only have power over my choices and not the choices of others. Therefore, I will take responsibility for my choices and trust the Lord to protect me from others' choices. It means that I look to myself first in taking responsibility for what has gone wrong, and for the lack of unity in my marriage or my home. Brokenness is putting flesh on humility. It does not blame others or defend self.

Brokenness is putting flesh on humility.
It does not blame others or defend self.

■ Mutual Submission

Mutual submission is the second—but equally essential—"rule of the road." Because the concept of biblical submission is so central to God's design for marriage and also enormously misunderstood by many of us as believers, I have treated it more extensively later in this book. However, it is also a critical component to our heart condition at the outset of building alignment in our marriages, which is why I'm bringing it up here.

Before discussing what biblical submission is, it is often more helpful to clarify what it is *not*. Many of us have a negative preconceived notion when we hear the word "submission." It often connotes slavery, fatalism, and the imbalance and abuse of power. Biblical submission, however, was designed by God and is therefore none of the above. Submission does not involve being a doormat, relinquishing our identity, or checking our brains at the door. In fact, submission is not any particular act(s). It is a heart condition that is not, in the first place, between two people. It is 100% between us and God.

Let me say that again: Submission is 100% between us and God. Only when this issue is settled between us and God does it have implications for our relationships and marriage. *Submission* is making the declaration at every turn,

---

"Lord, I trust YOU. You have me in Your hands
and You are in control no matter what."

That's what submission sounds like.

Submission is the highest form of faith. It puts everything in God's hands and trusts His authority structure for relationships and His sovereign control over those who trust him. A person operating in biblical submission really believes that God is in control, and especially that God is in control over those in authority over us.

Biblical submission also includes those in authority submitting to those beneath them. It is a heart condition of humility that allows for leaders to have a heart of submission to all those around them. The submission of leaders to those whom they lead is not to abdicate responsibility but to say, *"Lord, I trust that You can and do speak through those I am leading. I will constantly listen for Your voice in the things they are saying to me."* This is also and especially true of husbands and wives. It is why the Apostle Paul exhorts couples, not just wives, to be in submission to one another (Eph. 5:21-24). Submission is an issue of faith, not role—and the heart condition of faith is critical to a high octane marriage.

■ Mutual Engagement

One of the most common opposing forces to alignment in marriage that Amy and I observe in our work with couples is a lack of engagement. You'll remember this in the story of John and Megan. Often disengagement is either the result of hopelessness, passivity, and tiredness, or the failure to understand what level of energy and initiative it takes to build and maintain a high octane marriage.

Engagement is asking the question at every turn,

"Lord, what shall I do to forge unity here?"

That's what engagement sounds like.

Engagement is initiative. It never settles for unresolved conflict, disunity, or passivity. It is always paying attention to the status of the relationship and the heart condition of each spouse. It recognizes the importance of agreement and holds fast to preserving it.

■ The Dead End Road of DISunity

As I mentioned earlier, the opposites of brokenness, submission, and engagement are self-centeredness/pride, fear/control, and passivity. Let me tell you a story of what these heart issues can look like in a marriage—and their devastating results. Don't be hoodwinked by the fact that this story is nearly 3000 years old. Unfortunately, things haven't changed that much—at least with the human heart. Sure we've got faster chariots (called Porsches), but marriages are dealing with the exact same things. Perhaps we could try to learn something from other people's mistakes. This one is graphic.

The story starts with, *"(Ahab) not only considered it trivial to commit the sins of Jeroboam son of Nebat, but he also married Jezebel daughter of Ethbaal king of the Sidonians, and began to serve Baal and worship him."* Ahab and Jezebel's story ends with, *"There was never a man like Ahab, who sold himself to do evil in the eyes of the LORD, urged on by Jezebel his wife"* (see 1 Kings chapters 16 through 21). That's right. Ahab and Jezebel. What a pair! Doesn't sound like Ahab and Jezebel had much of a fairy tale marriage, does it?

God had told Ahab, the king of Israel, not to marry a foreign woman because she would bring idolatry into Israel's nation. But Ahab thought if he married the daughter of an enemy, the alliance would protect him from attack. So, Ahab ignored God's command and married Jezebel from Sidon, who worshiped idols. And Jezebel did exactly what God predicted: She ran the palace, tried to kill all of God's prophets (in which she was largely successful), bossed Ahab around, and opposed anyone who served the Lord. Ahab pretty much let Jezebel take over the kingdom. The result was idolatry, death, perversion, and eventually the complete annihilation of Ahab and all his relatives and friends— as well as a graphic elimination of Jezebel herself (2 Kin. 9:30-37).

Where did the problems in Ahab and Jezebel's marriage start?

1. Ahab was *afraid* of his enemies. He did not trust God's protection and provision. So he took matters into his own hands. His *fear and pride* compelled him into . . .

2. . . . *disobedience* and created a domino effect of destruction and devastation for Ahab and his family.

3. Then Ahab's fear led to *rebellion*, out of which he married a foreign woman against God's commandment.

4. Next, Ahab was *passive* in abdicating his throne to Jezebel, the daughter of his enemy, who then systematically began to destroy the kingdom.

5. In Ahab's passivity, Jezebel stepped in to take *control* and led the kingdom into idolatry and rebellion against God.

Ahab and Jezebel completely disregarded God's truth and His original design for them as individuals, for marriage, and for life in His kingdom. So God turned His anger upon Ahab and Jezebel, and they ultimately suffered a tragic death.

■ Unity against Fear, Control, Rebellion, and Passivity

It's not a pretty picture, is it? I wish I could say that these heart issues died with Ahab and Jezebel. Unfortunately, they are all too common—even today. Satan doesn't have to be particularly creative; the same old schemes seem to work in generation after generation of marriages. In fact, if you look closely at the real-life stories I've included in this book, you will likely see how the passivity-control cycle contributes to most if not all of them.

But that's not to say we have to let those schemes get the best of us. After all, the Apostle Paul said that we ought to be careful not to let Satan outwit us, because *"we are not unaware of his schemes"* (2 Cor. 2:11).

Men, are you aware of what passivity is—and what it looks like in *you?* Passivity in men is not simply "couch potato syndrome." A man can be physically active but personally and spiritually passive. Passivity in a man is a failure to stand his post as gatekeeper to protect and provide leadership for his wife and family. Passivity in men leads to fear in women who experience no protection or provision of leadership.

Women, are you aware of what control is, and what it looks like in *you?* Control is a common manifestation of fear, because control gives a false sense of security and safety. Therefore, where there is unresolved fear, wounding, or rejection, there is often control in various forms. Control is also a form of rebellion, because it disagrees with God about His government.

Rebellion and control allow the spirit of fear to unleash its intimidating and deadly power. Hence, we all too often see husbands who are afraid of their wives and wives who are calling all the shots. This deadly cycle usually begins with fear and rebellion in the form of passivity in men.

■ Unified Alignment

Active and godly leadership in men is one of the first steps of God's design for men and husbands. **Passivity opposes this design.** Passivity is a form of rebellion because it chooses to abdicate the God-designed role and responsibility of a man and a husband. As a parallel, a gentle and quiet spirit in women is one of the first steps of God's design for women and wives. **Control opposes this design.** Control is also a form of rebellion that refuses to trust God's government.

No matter what it looks like—passivity or control—God does not abide rebellion, as we saw in the story of Ahab and Jezebel. In fact, He openly opposes stiff-necked rebellion. That is the last thing I want—God's own hand opposing me. I want to be in alignment, don't you? I want full power under the hood and high performance on the road!

There are many more critical building blocks for a unified, aligned marriage, but overcoming the road blocks of rebellion, control, and passivity—exchanging them for brokenness, submission, and engagement—is usually the foundation of transforming all the others. Get freedom from these roadblocks—first in your own life and then in your relationship—and the other issues in the marriage (and in the individual partners) will be resolved much more easily.

TIME TO DRIVE—Personal Application Exercise for Couples

■ Agreeing on the Rules: Forging a Heart Condition for the Road Ahead

In this exercise, each spouse will have the opportunity to honestly assess the condition of his or her heart with respect to brokenness, submission, and engagement. It is important to give yourself plenty of time to work through this assessment. It is also important that where any conflict or hurt surfaces, both spouses stick with the process and work the assignment toward healing and reconciliation.

Some of the core issues opposing unity in your marriage may surface in this exercise. Please be assured that additional tools, truths, and exercises to address these issues thoroughly will be provided later on in the book. For this exercise it is important to get an honest assessment of the condition of heart.

1. In the posture of full engagement and tenderness, each spouse should start by telling the other, "I agree to learn and operate by the rules of mutual brokenness, mutual submission and mutual engagement even if I do not fully understand them at this point." If both of you were able to say that to each other, CONGRATULATIONS! You have put a stake in the ground with your first high octane agreement. You are now on the road. Now it is time to punch the gas.

2. Read each of the declarations on this list below, one at a time. Husbands, read the first declaration and respond as to whether the declaration is true for you. Then ask your wife if she agrees. Wives, read the same declaration and respond as to whether the declaration is true for you and ask your husband if he agrees.

    If the declaration is true about you and agreed upon by both spouses, check the box. If a particular declaration is not true, ask the question, "Is there any self-centeredness, control, fear, or passivity in my heart keeping me from living out this truth?" Ask the Lord to reveal areas of self-centeredness, control, and passivity that block unity and agreement in your marriage.

3. Confess all areas revealed; receive God's forgiveness. Use the 4R prayer model (see pages 41 and 42 if you need a reminder). When you get to the "rebuke" part of your prayer, verbally renounce any spiritual influence or topos (ground) of unforgiveness or shame in your life.

4. Fully repent and grant and receive forgiveness to one another.

Declarations:
- ❏ I look to my heart and my motives first when there is disagreement or tension.
- ❏ I look for my responsibility in disunity first.
- ❏ I race to repentance.
- ❏ I immediately forgive offenses or repeated patterns.
- ❏ I ask "Lord, what are you teaching me about me?"
- ❏ I am more interested in solutions and building unity than blame.
- ❏ I am more interested in my responsibility than my spouse's.
- ❏ I first pray for my spouse when I see he or she is not operating in his/her original design.
- ❏ I am fully submitted to my spouse and I trust the Lord with the outcome.
- ❏ I speak to my spouse with a gentle and quiet spirit (women).
- ❏ I speak to my spouse in an understanding way (men).
- ❏ I listen to the heart of my spouse before making decisions.
- ❏ I consult with my spouse on all important matters and believe that we make better decisions together.
- ❏ I think about ways to improve the unity in my marriage.
- ❏ I actively work on those areas that will contribute to unity in my marriage.
- ❏ I initiate conversations with my spouse on any issues that I feel stand "in between us."
- ❏ I initiate prayer with my spouse.
- ❏ I initiate one-on-one time with my spouse.
- ❏ I pay attention to the little things that bless my spouse and try to do them.

CHAPTER FOUR

Getting in Gear

For the Kingdom of God is not just fancy talk;
it is living by God's power.

1 CORINTHIANS 4:20

love that feeling of power—whether at the start of California Screamin' (the sweetest roller coaster at Disneyland's California Adventure), behind the wheel of a Porsche Carrara, or in the seat of my Ducati Monster motorcycle. In each case, the adrenalin, anticipation, expectation, and heart-pumping thrill are almost too much to bear—all because of the power I feel in my hands, my feet, or my back. It's fantastic.

Some may say I'm just a "thrill-seeker" or an "adrenalin junkie." Perhaps I am. But what I think is that I was designed for power. God designed power. God moves in power. God loves power. God's best work was the work of His power. The power of creation. The power over death and sin. Of course, His power is motivated by His love which is preeminent over all things. But His love expresses itself in power. The greatest expression of His love was His power on the cross. And here is the kicker: He gives His power to us!

Not too sure about that? Hang on!

■ More to Life than Meets the Eye

It should be becoming apparent to you as we move through this book together that there is more to your marriage than what you can see with your physical eyes. The "have a headache, take a pill" mentality just doesn't work for marriages. That's because you and your spouse are more than simply physical beings. You are also, by God's original design, spiritual beings. Therefore your marriage is subject to spiritual principles, spiritual issues, and even spiritual attack. You don't need a pill for stuff like that. You need real *power.*

Remember how on the day you were married, at some point during the ceremony—whether religious or civil—the person officiating said something like, "By the power invested in me by _____ (name of state, province, country, etc.), I now pronounce you man and wife." If you were married in a religious ceremony, the phrase "by God" was included. But whether it was or not, by virtue of the fact that marriage is God's design, your marriage IS in fact subject to the government and principles of two realms: that of earth and that of the heavenly (or spiritual) part of God's creation. It is crucial, therefore, that you have a thorough understanding and commitment to what the Bible says about this world—the fact that we live in one world with two realms and that we are affected by both.

The Scriptures tell us over and over again, start to finish, that though we see "one world" with our physical eyes, we really live in "two realms."[8] The natural realm is physical, and we interact with it based on our five senses: we see, we hear, we taste, we touch, and we smell. The other realm—the heavenlies spiritual realm—is spiritual. Most of us are not quite as comfortable interacting in that realm. Our spiritual senses are not generally as keenly developed as our physical ones—and understandably so.

In reality, the Scriptures teach that if you are a believing follower of Jesus Christ, your spirit has been made alive, regenerated from the state of spiritual death all human beings are in because of our sin. You are seated with Christ in the heavenly places in terms of position (Eph. 2:5-6). From a practical standpoint, you now have the *capacity* to operate in His delegated authority, hear the voice of His Spirit, and participate in His ministry with His love and power—that's life in the Kingdom!

I mention all this because I have come to recognize that it is very, very important for Christian couples to understand these principles and how they relate to marriage, specifically. Although we *perceive* our marriage issues in the natural realm (i.e. we experience them with our physical and emotional senses), they are very often, I believe, rooted in or at least influenced by the spiritual realm. After all, Scripture reminds us, *"For our struggle is not against flesh and blood, but against the rulers, against the authorities, against the powers of this dark world and against the spiritual forces of evil in the heavenly realms"* (Eph. 6:12).

■ Exercising our Spiritual Authority

In addition to the urgency of agreeing on the biblical worldview, Christian married couples need to know—and exercise—the authority that is theirs in both realms through Jesus Christ, and the power that comes with that authority. Yes, let me say that again. If you are in Christ, you have real power under the hood!

At the moment of salvation, every Christian is given new authority in God's economy. As those who are adopted as God's own children and marked by the name of Christ, we are seated with Christ in heavenly places and we carry the authority of Christ over all that opposes God (Eph. 2:5-6). To be seated with

Christ in the heavenly realms is to be united with Him in His seat of authority. His authority is universal and final. Because of His work on the cross and His grace to include us in that work, we carry His authority in His name.

Ephesians 1:19-22

I pray that you will begin to understand the incredible greatness of his power for us who believe him. This is the same mighty power that raised Christ from the dead and seated him in the place of honor at God's right hand in the heavenly realms. Now he is far above any ruler or authority or power or leader or anything else in this world or in the world to come. And God has put all things under the authority of Christ, and he gave him this authority for the benefit of the church.

Before we delve into the scope of the spiritual authority that God has delegated to us to exercise in our lives, our marriages, and our world, we need to have some understanding and agreement about the realm in which that authority operates. The Scriptures are clear that our world has two realms—natural and spiritual. The Scriptures are also clear on the point that there are both natural and spiritual forces that oppose God's design.

The natural forces of busyness, demands on our time and attention, preoccupations with family and household concerns, job and career pressures, entertainment, false comforts and indulgences, etc. all oppose God's design for marriage. The spiritual forces that oppose God's design for marriage are sin, demonic schemes and influences that seek to divide and discourage, lies that resemble the truth, and our reaction(s) to past hurts and wounds that have allowed demonic and destructive strongholds to develop and imprison us. We can address the natural forces with limited success; however, we must learn to exercise our God-given spiritual authority and power to defeat the spiritual forces, or we won't stand a chance of restoring our marriages to God's original design.

Ephesians 6:10-18

Be strong with the Lord's mighty power. Put on all of God's armor so that you will be able to stand firm against all strategies and tricks of the Devil. For we are not fighting against people made of flesh and blood, but against the evil rulers and authorities of the unseen world, against those mighty powers of darkness who rule this world, and against wicked spirits in the heavenly realms. Use every piece of God's armor to resist the enemy in the time of evil, so that after the battle you will still be standing firm. Stand your ground, putting on the sturdy belt of truth and the body armor of God's righteousness. For shoes, put on the peace that comes from the Good News, so that you will be fully prepared. In every battle you will need faith as your shield to stop the fiery arrows aimed at you by Satan. Put on salvation as your helmet, and take the sword of the Spirit, which is the word of God. Pray at all times and on every occasion in the power of the Holy Spirit. Stay alert and be persistent in your prayers for all Christians everywhere.

■ Getting Comfortable in the Seat of Power

In my experience over the past decade, the thought and language of spiritual warfare are among the biggest hindrances to believers experiencing God's life-giving freedom and transformation. This is particularly true in the Western culture, but not uncommon around the world.

Admittedly, many mistakes have been made regarding spiritual warfare. Spiritual warfare requires massive humility together with the proper and appropriate use of God's delegated power. Spiritual warfare can be dangerous. Because of these concerns (among others), many believers have chosen to mock it, marginalize it, disregard it, and diminish the reality of the existence of both a natural and spiritual realm. Honestly, we are much more comfortable with what we can see with our eyes. But such a life leaves no room for faith. I want my life—and my marriage—to be faith-filled, don't you? Faith is the currency of God's Kingdom. Without faith, the Bible says, it is *impossible* to please God (Heb. 11:6).

Sometimes the concept of spiritual warfare scares people, so they accuse those who believe in the biblical worldview of focusing too much on the devil. The biggest irony I find in this position comes through a simple reading of the life of Jesus in the Gospels. Jesus was constantly facing and referring to opposition in the spiritual realm. He was constantly engaging and dismantling the work of the devil. He was constantly casting out demons. And He did not reserve this work for himself, but also trained His disciples in the two realms and spiritual warfare, and sent them out to exercise His authority against the powers of darkness in the heavenly realms (Lk. 9:1-2, 10:18-19). What could be more biblical than doing the very things that Jesus did?

To many of us this worldview is distasteful, unsophisticated, and unscientific. After all, we are so much smarter in modern times than civilization was in the time of Christ, aren't we? We have plasma televisions, smart cars, iPhones, iPods, and iPads. If we are really that much smarter, though, why do we face the very same issues Jesus addressed in His time? In those days, people, relationships, marriages, communities, and nations were sick, broken, unfaithful, defeated, and spiritually opposed. Has that changed? Have our modern day smarts eliminated any of those realities? No. In fact, if anything, things are worse now than they were then. We may not be as smart as we think.

So here's the question facing us now, "How can we who profess to follow Jesus not also accept and operate in His worldview and training?" Do we have more wisdom than Jesus? Was Jesus lacking scientific and technological information? If medicine and science were as advanced in Jesus' time as they are today, would Jesus have changed His worldview? Would that have diminished Jesus' teaching on the natural and spiritual realms? Would that have eliminated His spiritual warfare training of disciples? Absolutely not. The Apostle John confirms that Jesus' world view was centered around two kingdoms in conflict:

1 John 3:8

But when people keep on sinning, it shows they belong to the Devil who has been sinning since the beginning. But the Son of God came to destroy these works of the Devil.

Jesus Himself often confirmed that the context of life on earth was set in a spiritual battle:

John 17:15-18

I'm not asking you to take them out of the world, but to keep them safe from the evil one. They are not part of this world any more than I am. Make them pure and holy by teaching them your words of truth. As you sent me into the world, I am sending them into the world.

If we choose psychology and sophistication to solve the problems in our lives and marriages, those will be our tools for transformation. We will be limited to our own natural discoveries, scientific and/or psychological advances, and behavioral modification techniques. Without any disrespect to the fields of medicine, psychology, and counseling—which all have significant contributions to make—in my experience, when it comes to personal and marriage restoration, these are like band-aids on bullet wounds. Beneath our anger, bitterness, unforgiveness, and hurts are spiritual roots that make room for the kingdom of darkness to oppress and imprison us. These spiritual roots are safe from the efforts of medicine, psychology and counseling. But they cannot prevail against the power, authority, and victory of the cross of Jesus Christ! His is the one and only power that can overcome the oppressive spiritual roots that knock us out of alignment with God's design. His is the one and only power that can restore our lives and marriages. And we have to exercise His power.

Galatians 4:3, 4, 7-9

And that's the way it was with us before Christ came. We were slaves to the spiritual powers of this world. But when the right time came, God sent his Son . . . to buy freedom for us who were slaves to the law, so that he could adopt us as his very own children . . . Now you are no longer a slave but God's own child. And since you are his child, everything he has belongs to you. Before you Gentiles knew God, you were slaves to so-called gods that do not even exist. And now that you have found God (or should I say, now that God has found you), why do you want to go back again and become slaves once more to the weak and useless spiritual powers of this world?

Alignment only happens when we believe and operate equally in both the spiritual and natural realms.

One of my good friends tells a poignant story about how recognition of the "one-world, two realms" truth dramatically transformed a marriage. Dave is a ministry leader who frequently travels around the world. This particular situation occurred in Puerto Rico in the home of a host pastor and his wife.

At Dave's first introduction to pastor Juan and his wife Carmela, it was obvious there were significant marital tensions, and there was no effort on their part to hide the difficulties. Dave and his team were to be there for one week ministering in Juan's and Carmela's church, staying in their home during that time. It was quickly setting up to be a long and awkward week.

Within hours after the team's arrival, Juan and Carmela readily confessed their marriage was hanging by a thread. They were exhausted in their marriage and voiced that they didn't know how much longer they could hang on. At that point, the effort to stay together was for the kids and the church.

Juan and Carmela were each carrying a great deal of emotional and spiritual baggage comprised of wounds from injustices along with insignificance and anger from various rejections in their early years. As Dave and his team ministered to Juan and Carmela, they quickly realized a couple of things. One was that the emotional and spiritual baggage each carried played against the other. It was as if the particular pieces of that "baggage" were buttons that, when pushed, launched each of them into a relational firestorm: the "buttons" of one pushed the buttons of the other person.

Secondly, and most importantly, Juan and Carmela recognized the spiritual component of their marriage—that they truly were not wrestling against flesh and blood (each other) but against evil spiritual beings (Eph. 6:12). Dave was somewhat startled when Juan jumped to his feet in the middle of a session and said, "Now I see it!" He had Carmela stand up opposite to him. He looked at Dave wide-eyed with excitement and said, "When Carmela and I are fighting, I need to ask Carmela to step to the side. I don't need to get at *her*. I need to get at the thing *behind* her and take authority over it!"

Juan laughed and said, "All this time I thought it was Carmela and me against each other, but all along there have been evil forces working against the both of us. We need to use the spiritual weapons we have learned about this week and stand united against the *real* enemy!"

At the end of Dave's week in Puerto Rico, Juan and Carmela were laughing and hugging each other. The greatest joy for everyone around them was how they as a couple were newly free to express love to each other and to their children, and to see the peace, joy, and laughter that came out of their family, all because they finally recognized who the *real* enemy was.

■ The Work Ethic Required to Exercise Power

We need to agree that our lives and marriages are lived in two realms, and exercise the power of Christ that lives in us. Operating in this kind of power in two realms requires an uncommon work ethic.

Operating in this kind of power in two realms requires an uncommon work ethic.

It requires complete agreement about what it takes to sustain our fight for a high octane marriage. I wish I could say that this kind of agreement is easy. It's simple, but it's not easy—and it takes two to achieve it. Mostly it takes time and energy and engagement. One hot spot for many marriages at this point is a disparate commitment level—that is, different views about how hard to work at alignment, how central the spiritual realm is, and how much time it takes to build and sustain biblical unity in marriage.

We know from our study of Genesis 2 and 3 that unity in marriage is God's design and therefore highly opposed. Sometimes this opposition even attacks the commitment and work ethic that we see in marriages. Below are some of the compromised work ethic and worldview philosophies we have seen functioning in marriages:

1. ASLEEP: *What do you mean "opposition?" Opposition to what?*
2. IN DENIAL: *We don't really have any secrets or spiritual issues and we are honest people.*
3. PASSIVE: *We try to fit it in when we have time, but there is so much going on.*
4. STRIVING: *We read, pray, alphabetize self-help books, and listen to last year's sermon CDs EVERY DAY in place of eating.*

We don't want any of the above to mark our marriages. What we DO want is a work ethic and worldview that parallel the work ethic and world view of Jesus. I believe Jesus had a high octane worldview and work ethic. He had an aggressive, intentional worldview which recognized that the critical element of spiritual, relational, and marital growth is *the state of our heart.*

The enemy wants to keep us either disengaged at the heart level or over-engaged at the achievement level. He, too, knows that our heart condition is crucial. His objective, however, is to leverage our heart condition *against* us — and against each other.

When we buy in to his lies, we are either not in the game or we cannot sustain an intense and intentional work ethic. We are either too hot or too cold. Too fast or too slow. What is needed, as modeled by Jesus, is sustained intensity and sustained intentionality.

A unified, agreed-on commitment to a biblical work ethic and worldview enables us to be in a position to sustain a high octane marriage, including asking:

- Do we both acknowledge and agree that the Bible is true today?
- Do we both acknowledge and agree that there are spiritual forces at work opposing our original design and that of our marriage?

These convictions will establish and sustain a spiritual work ethic that will sustain a high octane marriage. Anything less than this high octane approach will essentially be "compromised fuel"—you know, like the cheap stuff you get at those discount gas (or petrol) stations. Compromised fuel will cause our engine to sputter and our power to flutter. Maintaining a high octane marriage will require *action*, not just assent!

James 1:22-25

And remember, it is a message to obey, not just to listen to. If you don't obey, you are only fooling yourself. For if you just listen and don't obey, it is like looking at your face in a mirror but doing nothing to improve your appearance. You see yourself, walk away, and forget what you look like. But if you keep looking steadily into God's perfect law—the law that sets you free—and if you do what it says and don't forget what you heard, then God will bless you for doing it (emphasis added).

Philippians 3:12

I don't mean to say that I have already achieved these things or that I have already reached perfection! But I keep working toward that day when I will finally be all that Christ Jesus saved me for (emphasis added).

Colossians 1:28-29

So everywhere we go, we tell everyone about Christ. We warn them and teach them with all the wisdom God has given us, for we want to present them to God, perfect in their relationship to Christ. I work very hard at this, as I depend on Christ's mighty power that works within me (emphasis added).

■ Building Intensity and Intentionality

Achieving sustained intensity and intentionality takes training. Think of the marathoner, for instance. When she first starts to train, her intensity is kept at a slow pace. However, persistence, ritual, and discipline will build stamina, and her capacity to keep intensity at a greater pace will increase. The amount of training time it takes for a marathon runner to compete is extraordinary. It takes priority over everything else and her life is built around this training.

The key to developing a work ethic of intensity and intentionality is to build our lives around our hearts and their alignment with our Heavenly Father. Ask yourself the question, "What does it take for my heart to function in alignment with God's original design of truth and love—both for myself personally and for my marriage?" We know that living from our whole heart is central to Jesus' command because He tells us so. . . . *"Love the Lord your God with all your heart, soul, mind and strength and your neighbor as yourself"* (Mk. 12:30). He further declared that those who obey Him are the ones who love him and are His friends.

What might that look like in a marriage relationship? Below are a few key components to developing alignment with God's design for a work ethic marked by intensity and intentionality in our marriage:

■ 1. Agreement on the written Word

Maintaining and sustaining alignment in marriage can occur when each spouse loves to be in Scripture everyday. The heart condition here is joy and hunger. We don't just check it off the list, but we bathe in the joy of the Lord's wisdom and truth and love. We feel the need to be filled up with truth.

■ 2. Agreement on the living and spoken Word

The Holy Spirit will lead us into all truth (Jn. 16:13). It is by the power of the Holy Spirit that we hear God's voice, and that we are lead into the conviction and freedom of the truth. It is by the fruit of the Spirit that we can lovingly speak truth into each other. The heart condition here is that each spouse refuses to operate outside of the truth. We initiate honesty. We initiate speaking words of truth in love. We initiate speaking words of life and blessing.

■ 3. Agreement on building alignment in our hearts

There is nothing more fun and joyful than time with my wife. There is nothing more important than the unity of my marriage. Being together—and being in unity—is central to our relationship with Christ; it is central to our parenting; it is central to our discipleship and love of God; it is central and foundational to our effectiveness in God's Kingdom. The heart condition we're after here does not consider time spent connecting emotionally and spiritually as a chore or sacrifice. Why is it that so many of us feed our hearts only when we can fit it in around our activities?

■ 4. Running with Endurance

The marathoner will tell you that each marathon is different. Unexpected challenges spring up in each race. At the end of the day, there will be doubts about whether she can or wants to finish the race. In the end, only the commitment to hope and endure will see her through the overwhelming opposition to finishing the race.

There may be times in your marriage that you do not believe you can endure and finish. You do not see it. But as Amy and I have experienced, God IS faithful. He will see us (and you) through if we trust Him by enduring through times of chaos and challenge. Building agreement on a biblical work ethic and biblical worldview in your marriage will prepare you to endure to the finish line the race that God has set before you.

TIME TO DRIVE—Personal Application Exercise for Couples

■ Getting Into Alignment on Work Ethic

What gets in the way? Here are some of the major schemes we have seen compromise a "Jesus work ethic" and world view in marriages:

❏ Passivity
❏ Deception
❏ Entitlements
❏ Old tapes playing in our heads ("This is what I learned." "This is what was passed down to me.")

Now use this exercise as an opportunity to assess the work ethic and world view operating in your marriage. Check all that apply to you:

What does PASSIVITY sound like?

❏ I am too tired.
❏ I will do it tomorrow or this weekend.
❏ It is his/her turn—I just did it.
❏ I am entitled to some free time.
❏ I am entitled to some rest.
❏ He/she just doesn't understand everything else going on in my life.
❏ I will meet his/her needs when mine are met.
❏ I will exercise tomorrow.

What does DECEPTION sound like?

❏ It isn't that important.
❏ If I miss one day of Scripture reading—no big deal.

❑ This or that is more pressing than praying with my spouse; we can do that later.

❑ She needs to just serve me all the time, that is what the Bible says. It is my right.

❑ Television will help me relax and unwind.

❑ I will rest on the couch for 10 minutes and then exercise.

❑ This cheesecake will give me more energy.

❑ I can't get away with my spouse or take him/her on a date; the kids need me.

❑ The more activities we and our kids are involved in—THE BETTER!

What do ENTITLEMENTS sound like?

❑ I am entitled to a little down time.

❑ I know someone else will do it.

❑ I have worked hard all week, I deserve some alone time with myself and my TV (or shopping, eating, etc.)

What do OLD TAPES sound like?

❑ This is how Mom and Dad did it.

❑ I never saw dad clean a dish, wash a toilet, or change a diaper—that is women's work.

❑ Dad did all of the bills; Mom wasn't involved in any of the planning.

❑ Yelling at each other in front of the kids is normal.

❑ My parents never took the time to be alone together.

❑ We never had meals together; we were too busy.

Where are you and your spouse when it comes to forging a common work ethic? Temperament and family of origin have a lot to do with how you will approach this topic. Be honest and accepting of one another's views, while at the same time cognizant that what seems "normal" to you may not be healthy (or biblical).

Without going to either extreme—passivity ("I'm okay, you're okay; let's just muddle through") or accusation ("I'm right; you're wrong; you just need to do it my way")— talk with your spouse about the above inventory. Check any boxes that apply to you. Together, pray through any of the above obstacles to sustaining a strong and mutual work ethic in your marriage:

1. Get back into the posture of full engagement and tenderness—knee to knee, hand in hand, eye to eye.

2. Each person, husbands going first, can "pray through" the items he or she checked on the work ethic inventory. Use the 4R prayer (see pages 41-42) model as a guideline for your prayer.

3. Verbally and specifically extend forgiveness to one another.

4. Together, make a spiritual declaration of your commitment to live in a biblical worldview and work ethic.

    ⇒ You WILL overcome every spiritual scheme against your marriage.

    ⇒ You WILL exercise your authority in Christ.

    ⇒ You WILL receive the power of God's Holy Spirit to empower and sustain you.

    ⇒ You WILL endure to the end and have the strength and power to do all that God has designed and called you to do!

Designed
for Alignment

I n Section One we explored the truths that unlock God's high octane power in our lives and marriages:

> Alignment with our Original Design
> Authentic Repentance
> Immediate Forgiveness
> A Jesus World View
> An Uncommon Work Ethic

In this section, we will discover how to apply that power to our lives and marriages for permanent transformation—alignment with God's original design.

We need the power of God's Holy Spirit to empower transformation in our lives, and to sustain it. We can't make our marriages run powerfully on our own steam any more than we can make a car or motorcycle operate by our own leg-work. Imagine trying to run on a treadmill that has no power—that's hard work! Then imagine plugging in the treadmill and being able to run at top speed with much less effort. That's the beauty of power. In this chapter, we'll learn about how to appropriate and handle God's high octane power to transform our marriage, and how to sustain it. Here, we will engage in the truths of:

> First Ministry
> Speaking the Truth in Love
> Overcoming Strongholds
> Being a Team

The exercises in this section will be more challenging and grow in intensity and time commitment. Are you ready for the ride?

CHAPTER FIVE

Horsepower and Torque

For if a man cannot manage his own household,
how can he take care of God's church?

1 TIMOTHY 3:5

've learned that exhilaration comes from acceleration and acceleration comes from horsepower and torque. "I feel the need, the need for speed!" exclaimed Tom Cruise in the movie *Top Gun*. I love that line.

Working together, horsepower and torque make for an awesome ride. One without the other, however, results in discouragement and disappointment. All horsepower and no torque is like riding a ten-speed bicycle uphill in tenth gear. All torque and no horsepower is like riding that ten-speed downhill in first gear. In each case, there is no speed, no power, and no acceleration—just immediate and sustained exhaustion.

In His wisdom, God gave us "horsepower and torque" so that we can experience the exhilarating acceleration of living in alignment with God's perfect design in our marriage. We find it when—like a cyclist—we discover that "sweet spot" of balance between speed and resistance.

■ The Need for Balance

Very few people knew that Antonio's wife was dying and his child was struggling with whether to go on living. What everyone did know was that he was a prominent member of the community. They knew what a positive influence he'd had in the lives of kids and families in his community for the past three decades. He loved the Lord and poured his life into the people around him. His work and ministry to other people in the community absorbed his time and energy and passion. He loved what he was doing. Everyone around him was thriving—his career, his results, his ministry for the Lord, his accolades from others, and his place in the world.

Upon learning of his wife and child's critical condition, Antonio's close friends made the observation that something wasn't adding up. Life *outside* the family seemed to be thriving, while life *inside* the family was barely surviving. But Antonio didn't see it. It wasn't until he experienced a direct confrontation with his family's health that his eyes were opened and he realized no one was guarding the gate to his family. This revelation led to the understanding that none of his great work in the community meant anything if he lost his family. He was suddenly aware of the massive hypocrisy of speaking as an authority and mentor into the lives of kids and families when his own marriage and family were crumbling around him.

To Antonio's credit, he chose to reorder his priorities and make his marriage and family his *first ministry*—to lead his wife and child and get his own home in order. He immediately went to work as the gatekeeper of his family and provided the God-designed leadership his family needed. Today, his wife and child are healthy and thriving and he has enormous spiritual authority in speaking into the lives of others.

This is not an unusual story in my experience. But in circumstances like these, where alignment with our first ministry is not pursued, the outcome is usually tragic.

"First ministry" is the term Amy and I appreciate and use to describe the biblical principle that marriage and family are the primary arena where our love for and obedience to God are tested. God designed marriage to be a powerful representation of His glory and unity. This is such a dynamic concept that He used marriage throughout the New Testament Scriptures as a graphic illustration of the honor, commitment, and unselfish love that is to exist between Jesus Christ and the Church (Eph. 5:25-27).

I firmly believe that, in order to experience the power of God's design for marriage, alignment with the principle of first ministry is essential. It is alignment with the truth of "first ministry" that leads to horsepower and torque. When we really start living out this biblical principle, a spiritual transaction occurs. We begin to experience the release of God's power and His favor starts to blow through our marriage. We begin to experience supernatural acceleration in our unity and, man, is it exhilarating! In our observation, here a few examples of the kind of power "first ministry" alignment in marriage generates:

- power to maintain unity under attack
- power to see, sustain, and encourage each family member in God's original design for him or her
- power to overcome the schemes of the enemy
- power to overcome injustices and unforgiveness
- power to overcome hurts
- power to overcome destructive patterns
- power to overcome love deficits

- power to overcome challenges
- power to raise joyful, secure, obedient, and capable children
- power to restore other marriages
- power to advance God's Kingdom because of being in alignment with God's truth.

Amy and I saw radical transformation through these "first ministry" truths in the lives of a couple named Jonathan and Kate. When we first met them, they seemed to be the perfect couple. They had it all: beautiful children, a wonderful home, and great friends. To look at them one would think they were joyful, content, and thriving. Jonathan was a successful businessman and Kate held the prize for "the woman who could do it all." She was classroom mom at school, an elder in her church, and volunteered in numerous positions throughout their community. She loved the fast-paced adrenaline rush from all that she was doing and she loved the praise she received from everyone around her. Jonathan and Kate were committed to all the "good things" to which they volunteered their time. They gave sacrificially and provided excellent leadership in a number of capacities.

What people didn't see was the chaos and stress that reigned at home. Because Kate poured out so much to the community, she had nothing left to pour into her family. Her house, she admits now, was unorganized. Chaos reigned. She prepared meals only one or two times a week and they ate out the other nights. She had no devotional time with the Lord because she allowed no quiet time. Life was one event after another. She fell into bed exhausted every night thinking, "Why aren't other women pulling their weight?"

At the same time, Jonathan did not have the Lord's eyes for Kate and her priorities. Kate did not know the Lord's heart for her and which activities were authorized by Him and which were not. All this came to a screeching halt when Kate's adrenals said "no more" and she came down with a six-month long illness that left her bedridden and unable to do anything.

It was during that time that the Lord began doing an amazing work of bringing Jonathan and Kate into alignment with His design for them as a married couple. Out of a necessity to survive, together they clung to Jesus because Kate's life depended on it. Jonathan cancelled months of work to sit by her bedside. He read Scripture to her for hours on end and they began praying together and seeking the Lord's heart on everything. Jonathan stepped into his position as gatekeeper of the house and for the first time was really leading. His eyes were on his household and he became committed to ensuring that everything that took place was honoring to and authorized by the Lord. Jonathan also learned to exercise his spiritual authority and to battle demonic attack through spiritual warfare when he perceived it coming against his family.

For the first time, Kate began to experience the peace of God. She began to thrive spiritually, even though her physical body was still weak. She made a full recovery and what emerged was a transformed couple.

By God's grace and Jonathan and Kate's obedience, both passivity and pride were demolished and "first ministry" was established in their household. Now Jonathan leads his family, Kate partners with him, and they seek the Lord daily for His will and submit all activities to Him. There is a supernatural peace in their home. It is the kind of home you can enter on any day and find peace, warmth, order, and amazing hospitality. Through their obedience they now produce supernatural, life-changing, power-packed fruit—all of which they joyfully and generously share.

Jesus came with power and authority to restore people and marriages, as Jonathan and Kate's (and Antonio's) stories graphically illustrate. Jesus gave that power and authority to His Church and His disciples—including us—that His Kingdom might continue to advance and change the world. But we have largely forgotten that important truth. We have forgotten that we are the hands and feet of Jesus. We have forgotten that we possess the Spirit, power, and authority of God to bring healing and restoration to the world. We have also forgotten, perhaps most importantly, that in order to effectively be God's instruments of power and healing and restoration in the world, we must first be healed and restored *ourselves*.

We wrote this book primarily out of the same conviction and truth the Apostle Paul was instilling in Timothy as the apostles were establishing the early Church and its leadership (see 1 Timothy 3). As Paul was training the first churches, he instructed Timothy about the character required of a leader in the Church: *"For if a man cannot manage his own household, how can he take care of God's church"* (1 Tim. 3:5)?

This is a great question, and perhaps a more important one now than ever before. The world is a broken place filled with broken people, broken marriages, broken families, broken leaders, broken communities, and broken nations. Sadly, in many ways the Church of Jesus Christ is indistinguishable from the rest of the world in this regard. Worse still, the leadership of the Church (the very ones to which the above Scripture passage speaks) often lives in the same condition. Granted, it may not appear so, but if we dare to look just below the surface, we will likely find weariness, discouragement, deception, disillusionment, and buried crisis in many Christian marriages and families.

The truth of Paul's exhortation to Timothy applies to every disciple who intends to do the work of ministry in the name of the Jesus Christ. I feel strongly about the broad application of this truth for two reasons. First, this truth is in place to foster alignment in the Kingdom; that is, to get us in line or "in sync" with God's original design for life. I use the term "Kingdom" here as a synonym for the true "Church," and to avoid the constricting connotation that the Church is confined to a building. Kingdom leaders reach far beyond walls of the churches in our communities. Yet by and large we have narrowly defined ministry leadership as vocational pastors. The reality is that we find ministry leaders all over our communities: in business, law, education, medicine, construction, service, politics, etc. There are ministry leaders in every occupation and calling. Because of this, I like the term "Kingdom" rather than "Church," in order to include Christians from every walk of life. In his exhortation to Timothy, Paul provides deep insight into the priorities of those who would lead in the Kingdom. But the very nature of this truth makes it a healthy paradigm for *all* believers.

Secondly, I believe this truth is desperately needed in the Church based upon my personal experience with Church (or Kingdom) leaders and volunteers. I'm confident I'm not the only one who has observed that many people neglect their marriages and families in the name of "serving the Lord." Somehow many have "baptized" church work and ministry as the highest priority in each believer's life—making it an idol instead of an act of service. Paul's truth of "first ministry" flies in the face of that lie.

On the other hand, some families fall into the opposite trap of making the family itself an idol. I've seen this happen time and time again where the children's schedules and desires—not the Lord's—drive the marriage. Paul's truth of "first ministry" flies in the face of that lie, too. Managing one's household well, as Paul put it in his letter to Timothy, includes keeping both ministry and family in balance with God's original design. Drifting to either extreme can actually lead to a form of idolatry:

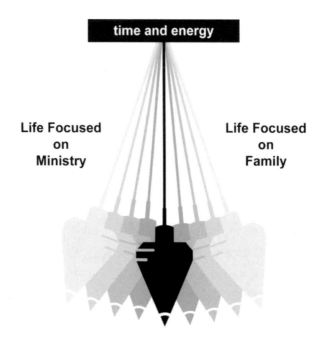

How many church leaders are facing a marriage or family crisis? How many ministry leaders are facing a marriage or family crisis and *don't know it*? How many pastors and teachers are dealing with parenting issues that compromise their integrity and authority? How many spouses of those in ministry are miserable and unfulfilled? Why are the statistics on marriage among believers so similar to marriages in the secular world?

None of us who are married and invested in Kingdom life and ministry are exempt from Paul's exhortation for leaders. God's vision for His Kingdom is that *every* believer would become a disciple, and that every disciple has been sent by Jesus into mission and ministry. This means that God has designed every one of His children to live in alignment with His truth and to exercise His power, love, and authority for His Kingdom purposes. Look carefully at Jesus' commissioning of His first disciples and those who would follow in faith:

Matthew 28:18-19

Jesus came and told his disciples, "I have been given complete author-ity in heaven and on earth. Therefore, go and make disciples of all the nations, baptizing them in the name of the Father and the Son and the Holy Spirit."

Mark 16:15

And then he told them, "Go into all the world and preach the Good News to everyone, everywhere."

Luke 24:47

With my authority, take this message of repentance to all the nations, beginning in Jerusalem: "There is forgiveness of sins for all who turn to me."

John 17:18, 20

As you sent me into the world, I am sending them into the world. . . . I am praying not only for these disciples but also for all who will ever believe in me because of their testimony.

In each of these gospel accounts of Jesus, we learn two important truths. First, Jesus sent His disciples into the world, armed with His power, authority, and commissioning to carry on His ministry. Secondly, He intended for that directive to apply to all disciples who would ever believe in Him. Based upon these two truths consistently recorded by all of the Gospels, it is apparent that there is a significant calling on each believer to the mission and ministry of Jesus Christ. In this respect, there is little difference between elders, deacons, and all disciples. Elders and deacons may have specific oversight responsibilities, but each one of us has ministry responsibilities, credibility, and spiritual authority to cultivate and protect.

For followers of Jesus Christ, regardless of whether or not we are elders or deacons, homemakers or businessmen, lawyers, doctors, tradesmen, pastors, or teachers, the principle of "first ministry"—putting our marriage and family first—is critical to the effectiveness of our ministries.

We cannot reasonably expect to excel in life and ministry if our marriage and family are out of order, either by neglecting them or by idolizing them.

Marriage and family are God's foundational building blocks for life as He designed it. Therefore, for those who are married, the health of your marriage must take first priority over everything. If it doesn't, everything else—including your children, leadership, discipleship, ministry efforts, credibility, and spiritual authority—will suffer.

Can I just reaffirm that God designed marriage to be exciting and powerful? God designed marriage to be central both to creation and to the healthy sustenance of life. And because God made it so integral, we should make it our top priority. I believe one of the best ways we can advance the Kingdom of God is to invest in the health of marriages so that the ministry of Jesus Christ will be marked with joy and power. We need horsepower and torque!

Think about these questions:

What if each husband and father functioned as the pastor to his family *first*? That is, what if he focused his attention on building a high octane marriage and on raising up the next generation in God's design *first*?

What if each wife and mother focused her attention on building alignment with God's design in her heart and prioritizing her husband and children *first?* What if those in ministry understood that their authority in Christ and in the Church was dependent upon their integrity with this truth? It's simple — the Church would be reformed! The Church would begin to rediscover its original design for life in the Kingdom.

This is exactly what Ben and Amanda experienced. A few days before Ben was to start his last year of seminary, Amanda told him their marriage would not survive another year, the way they had been living. Ben had been traveling two hours by train to seminary for half the week, and when home he was entirely engulfed in his studies and internship. Getting his Master of Divinity degree was something he had dreamed of doing since rededicating his life to Jesus in the eighth grade.

Once Ben realized his wife was dead serious, they called to meet with Amy and me. In that meeting it became painfully clear to Ben that he needed to either quit seminary or run the risk of his marriage failing altogether. While the two of them would have said that God was first in their lives, their marriage relationship did not reflect that. In fact, they had put ministry first—before God.

Finally, through tears, Ben convinced Amanda that she did come before seminary in his priorities, and he would quit his lifelong dream to prove it. Almost all of their friends, professors, and family thought it was a mistake.

Ben and Amanda both realized they had parts to play in moving their marriage out of the hole it was in. While they repented to God and one another, asking for and granting forgiveness that day, they recognized there was an even more intense season of commitment ahead. It would take a great deal of grace, effort, and follow-through to reverse the effects of three years of living completely disconnected and in their own worlds.

We gave them homework for the next several months. As part of their assignment, we required them to spend three hours a night sitting face to face and talking to each other. Ben described their first efforts as "some of the most awkward times of conversation and silence we experienced. When you're that disconnected, what on earth do you talk about for three hours . . . let alone 15 hours a week for many weeks in a row? It was hard work but we were desperate for change, so we went after it."

In the months to follow, God started showing Ben and Amanda the sources of their disunity. Their hearts were tainted with fear, mistrust, control, insecurity, passivity, self-centeredness, independence, and more. Ben was frozen in passivity, walking on eggshells around sensitive topics which he was afraid to address to avoid spiraling down into dissension. For her part, past years of being disappointed and abandoned by significant men in her life had left Amanda's heart calloused and afraid to trust Ben.

Their marriage was marked by arguments, frustration, and resentment and they would often lock horns for control in the marriage. Being raised by a single mother much of her childhood, Amanda's attitude was that she "would not be walked upon." Just the opposite, Ben's attitude was "what the man says, goes." Working together as a team to come to agreement as part of the mutual submission process was foreign to them.

But today, to anyone who asserts that a marriage like theirs is hopeless, Ben and Amanda now say, "There is hope! You don't have to stay stuck in the rut. Our marriage, while we are still growing, is now marked by peace! No more crazy, all-out fights, no more walking on eggshells, no more silent treatment or withholding."

Walking in alignment with God's design for marriage has brought them absolute life. The principle of "first ministry" has borne its intended fruit in their marriage and in their ministry life. Four years later Ben finished his master's degree and a few years after that entered into full-time ministry. This was the very dream God had planted in Ben's heart years before — only this time it looked dramatically and delightfully different. Now trust had been built. Amanda gave Ben her blessing and they jumped into ministry as a team. Their marriage and family are marked by peace and joy and they have sustained alignment even under the demands of full-time pastoring and occupational ministry.

Life in the Kingdom, Jesus said, is "life in abundance" (Jn. 10:10). This means we can (and should!) be experiencing the life-giving power and unity that God designed for marriage and family relationships. Marriage in God's Kingdom is filled with joy and power and life and laughter. God has ordained and designed marriage in His Kingdom to handle every storm of life with strength, composure, unity, and victory. The truths about how to have an aligned marriage—the truths I am sharing with you in this book—are not new; in fact, they are ancient. But they are tested, true, and biblical, though largely forgotten. My prayer and strong desire is for these truths to transform marriages where there are hearts that are hungry to grow and change—like Ben and Amanda—and that are hungry to experience the life, power, peace, and joy that God designed in marriage.

TIME TO DRIVE—Personal Application Exercise for Couples

1. Sitting in the posture of full engagement and tenderness, consider the following list. For each item, privately assess on a scale of 1-10 (with 10 being the best) your present commitment to "first ministry." Each of you write down two numbers, one for your self-assessment and one assessing your spouse.

2. Share your answers one item at a time. Deal with any necessary repentance and forgiveness between you and God and each other.

3. Develop agreement about your plan going forward to establish and sustain the truth of first ministry in your lives. Write it down and follow through. At the end of the list I will provide a sample plan for your review.

■ First Ministry Assessment

_____ _____ I feel completely connected to my spouse emotionally.

_____ _____ I feel completely connected to my spouse spiritually.

_____ _____ I feel completely connected to my spouse physically.

_____ _____ I initiate time every day to connect deeply with my spouse.

_____ _____ After my relationship with the Lord, my marriage is my highest priority.

_____ _____ I initiate time every day to connect deeply with each of my kids.

_____ _____ My spouse and I pray together every day.

_____ _____ My spouse and I speak truth and words of life to each other constantly.

_____ _____ I am constantly paying attention to whether my spouse is living in his/her original design.

_____ _____ I bless my spouse every day.

_____ _____ I plan my day in order to have time to deeply connect with my spouse (whether physically at home or traveling)

_____ _____ I am constantly seeking the Lord about how to align with and fulfill my God-designed role in my marriage.

_____ _____ I make necessary personal sacrifices in order to prioritize time with my wife and family.

_____ _____ I respond immediately to requests made by my spouse.

_____ _____ I have my home in order. Chaos has been replaced by peace and joy.

_____ _____ I crush hypocrisy by having my home in order.

_____ _____ I do not allow circumstances (job, ministry, outside demands) to steal peace in my home.

_____ _____ I keep my home in order so that we have time and energy to follow and serve the Lord.

■ Sample First Ministry Plan

1. We will pray together every day, seeking the Lord for direction, speaking the truth in love, and staying deeply connected.
2. We will spend time together every day connecting emotionally, spiritually, and physically.
3. We will pray for and with (and connect deeply with) our kids every day.
4. We will have our home in order and at peace before making other commitments.
5. We will seek to have our home in order so that we have time and energy to serve the Lord.
6. We will check in with each other constantly to make sure we are in agreement and unity on all things.
7. We will not commit to anything without complete agreement and alignment first.
8. We will seek to commit only to things we can do as a couple or a family as much as possible.

CHAPTER SIX

The Sweet Sound

Speaking the truth in love,
we will in all things grow up
into him who is the Head, that is, Christ.

EPHESIANS 4:15

I asked Jack to look into his wife Nancy's eyes and speak words of blessing to her for 15 seconds. 15 seconds! Silence. He could not find a single word to say. It wasn't because he didn't feel blessing and favor for his wife. It wasn't because of anger or unforgiveness. This was a man who loved his wife; he had just never learned to express his heart in words. It required too much vulnerability.

This experience is not uncommon. Few of us are trained to speak from our hearts. Even fewer of us are trained to be able to speak words of life, truth, and blessing for 15 seconds without stopping. Amy and I love this exercise because when we do it with couples, we get to watch their hearts be unlocked and see the waterfall of love, life, and favor start to flow.

■ The Heart behind the Words

One of the things that lights me up is the sweet sound of power, whether it is the deep rumble of a Harley Davidson, the smooth tones of my Ducati monster, or the supersonic boom of a fighter jet just above my head. It makes me smile and pump my fist. "Sweet music," I say to my friends. Interestingly, I get the same feeling when I watch a husband open up his heart and speak out of that heart for his wife. There is nothing more manly than the sweet sound of truth in love.

My experience is that speaking the truth in love is an art that is rarely understood and therefore rarely taught. However, we can learn to create that "sweet sound" in our own marriages, whether we've done it up to this point or not. I know from personal experience that couples can rebuild and grow their relationship by learning to speak words of life into one another. Speaking the truth in love is the sweet sound of healing and restoration and life.

God has created us with the capacity to discern the fragrance of each other's hearts. When we speak, we can either give off the aroma of the kingdom of heaven, or the kingdom of hell itself. As children of God, and brothers and sisters in Christ, our tongues are designed to be used to *bless*.

James 3:9-12

With the tongue we praise our Lord and Father, and with it we curse men, who have been made in God's likeness. Out of the same mouth come praise and cursing. My brothers, this should not be. Can both fresh water and salt water flow from the same spring? My brothers, can a fig tree bear olives, or a grapevine bear figs? Neither can a salt spring produce fresh water.

However, when we speak from a heart condition that is other than faith and blessing—say of fear, pride, or a critical spirit, for example—the words and thoughts we communicate are energized by the spiritual kingdom with which they are aligned, in this case that of the enemy.

James 3:6

And tongue is a flame of fire. It is full of wickedness that can ruin your whole life. It can turn the entire course of your life into a blazing flame of destruction, for it is set on fire by hell itself.

When we speak from a heart condition of faith, blessing, and hope, on the other hand, those words are also energized by the Kingdom they are aligned with — God's Kingdom.

Speaking truth from the heart in love releases God's power for reconciliation, trust, healing, and forgiveness. Both the spoken words and the accompanying heart condition are required for God's power to be released. The words must be spoken aloud because God's words of power are spoken aloud.

God spoke the world into existence. Jesus spoke out loud when operating in the two realms in His ministry on earth. Evidently, God's economy is founded on the power of the spoken word. Both the natural and the spiritual realms are privy to the things we say out loud and the things we say have spiritual implications. Words of truth and life have the power to advance God's Kingdom. Words of deception and destruction have the power to oppose God's Kingdom. Literally, the Bible teaches, the power of life and death is in the tongue (Prov. 18:21).

■ **Speaking the Truth in Love**

There may be nothing more powerful and transforming we can do than speaking the truth in love. It is part of our maturing in Christ. It is part of demonstrating His heart, life, and Spirit in us. I believe it is so threatening to the powers of darkness that evil forces make every effort to cause us to err on the side of an overdose of truth at the expense of love—or the converse, an overdose of love at the expense of the truth. Here, again, we need *balance*. The key to transformation and alignment in both the speaker and listener is 100% truth and 100% love without withholding either component. In talking about building marriages in alignment with God's design, I think this particular training from Paul is a key to maturity and growth in marriage:

Ephesians 4:15-16

But speaking the truth in love, we must grow up in every way into him who is the head, into Christ, from whom the whole body, joined and knit together by every ligament with which it is equipped, as each part is working properly, promotes the body's growth in building itself up in love.

The need to speak the truth in love is usually prompted when we observe someone we love participating in conduct or speech that is out of alignment with God's design for him or her, or out of alignment with God's truth or character. When this occurs, that person needs to hear the truth in order to break free from the lies he or she has started to believe. The caution here is that if the truth is delivered without pure love, it is much less likely to be heard. Instead it can create wounding instead of the encouragement and godly correction or exhortation that was intended.

In marriage, God's design for communication includes delegating to us the obligation to speak the truth in love whenever we observe our spouse operating outside of his or her original design. One of the challenges of this responsibility is that it requires us to have God's heart and not merely our own. There is no room for any impurity or self-centeredness. When Amy and I are confronted with this "opportunity" (i.e. one or both of us sees something in the other that is out of alignment), we have learned to ask the following question to help us make sure our hearts and motives are pure:

What does it look like to reflect God's heart when delegated to speak truth in love?

Here's what we've learned:

1. Initiate seeking God's heart

When I first observe conduct or speech in Amy that warrants a truth response (i.e. some way in which she is operating outside of her original design), I immediately go to prayer and seek God's heart on the matter. **I seek to maintain ZERO tolerance for SELF.** That is, I must care more that truth be spoken in love than that I get my point across or vent my feelings. The smallest fraction of SELF will contaminate both truth and love — like "dog-doo cookies."

Haven't you ever heard of dog-doo cookies? My friend John tells a hilarious story about a teenage boy who came home after school and announced to his mom that he and his friend wanted to go see an "R rated" movie. They admitted it had only a very short sexual scene and four or five curse words in it — not a lot of sin, just a little. The mother said they could go if they really felt it was worthwhile, but there was one condition: They had to stay and have some of the chocolate chip cookies she was baking before they went. The kids were excited about the treat until they heard their mother's final comment, "In the batch of cookies I've mixed in a little dog-doo. Just a little bit, not enough to change the taste of the cookies or their texture."

The point was well-taken. The teenagers declined the cookies — and the movie.

The same is true for us and our heart condition. The slightest infiltration of sin and self contaminates the whole thing. What that means is that I cannot allow even a little of my own selfishness, irritation, busyness, or laziness to contaminate my response to Amy. For example: My wife seems not at peace, distracted or anxious. I smell FEAR. Fear is one of the key schemes against women to take them out of their original design (which is fearless and faith-filled). Rather than simply saying . . .

"Don't be afraid, it will all work out," or
"I can't believe you are choosing fear," or
"Don't you trust me to handle this?" or
"Where is your faith?"

. . . before I spout off, I must go to prayer to seek God's heart on the issue and get my heart in alignment with His:

"Lord, what are You teaching me about me?"
"What is Your heart and truth on this issue and at this time?"

I need to have the heart of Christ, which carries the perfect balance and bouquet of truth and love. I need to be broken of self and self-interest, and be *for* my wife and her victory. Until my heart is submitted to the Lord's, I don't speak. This can occur in a matter of a split-second or sometimes it takes weeks.

Sometimes the truth is clear but I am not at peace in being able to deliver it in the love of Christ. This is sometimes triggered by fear, control, or an over-investment in the "right" response. Peace must rule in my heart before I speak. My goal is to be in constant intimacy with Christ such that I can speak truth in love at the ready.

2. Initiate speaking God's truth in love

When I observe conduct or speech that warrants a truth response, it is unacceptable to overlook it or ignore it. By my recognition of it, God is providing an opportunity for growth and maturity for me and my wife and our marriage. **I seek to have ZERO tolerance for PASSIVITY.** By overlooking or ignoring deception, false conclusions, or anything less than original design, I open the door to rebellion to reign in my home. Rebellion is the satanic objective. Submission and obedience are God's design for His children. When an opportunity for life and truth presents itself, my obedient and submissive response to the Lord is to reflect His heart, which can be characterized as speaking the truth in love.

The biblical story of Jonah is an excellent example of what happens when God asks us to reflect His heart and we refuse. Jonah ran the other way and ended up sitting for three days in the dark, smelly belly of a whale to think about what the right response *should* have been. I certainly don't want to elicit that kind of corrective action from the Lord—do you?

■ Staying at the Table

So get up and go! The question isn't "if" we say something; it is "when" and "how." The key is the heart condition of *tenacity*. That means staying with the issue until it is settled. By "staying with the issue" I mean that I plan to stay in communication with my spouse in tender and gentle ways until we understand each other and have agreement on the action steps moving forward. It also means paying attention to my own heart condition until I am ready to speak— and then speaking. Then, once I have spoken, it means staying in conversation on the issue until there is peace, healing, and agreement between us.

The importance of the practice of "staying at the table" cannot be over-stated. Most marriages that end do so because one or both people were unwilling to stay at the table of discussion through the frustration, exasperation, impatience, discouragement, distrust, etc.—essentially, all of the various phases and emotions we go through when we are working things out. Most important of all is not to give up, not to walk away.

3. Insist on original design

The content of speaking truth in love is original design. If we limit ourselves to speaking only original design, our spouses will experience truth in love. Original design is the simplest and most powerful way to speak truth in love. But doing so requires knowing three things:

1) God's design for marriage
2) God's design for wives/husbands
3) God's design for *my* wife/husband

When these design truths are inscribed on my mind and heart, I am then equipped to discern when they are NOT operating. In other words, by knowing what the truth is and what it looks like, I can readily tell when it is not happening. The key is to know the truth (God's original design). That is why we started in Chapter One by discussing and exploring God's design for marriage and for each spouse.

Anything less than original design is bondage in some form or degree. **I seek to have ZERO tolerance for BONDAGE.** Consider this: How loving is it to observe my spouse in emotional and spiritual distress and simply stand by and watch? I need to know (and be convinced of) what it is that exposes chains of sin— the Truth. Then, what is it that breaks the chains of sin? It is the love of Christ, and the power of the blood which represents how great His love is for us. When I help my wife (or anyone else, for that matter), break those chains and move freely into operating in her original design, I demonstrate the love of Christ for her.

I want to emphasize again at this point the need for a posture of humility and selflessness in this exercise. There is great opposition to the transactional power of speaking the truth in love. It is so easy for self and sin to get in the way. We have to guard our hearts against:

- the need to be right
- a critical spirit
- harshness
- control
- self-righteousness
- legalism
- pride

Speaking the truth in love requires us to insist on **speaking only original design** and not permitting ourselves to let our SELF in by the "back door" through venting, retaliation, harshness, or shame. An example of hurtful "back door" truth is, "Honey, God made you fearless; you are not a trembling, anxious, worry-wart," or "I don't care what anybody says; your heart is not wicked." We want to avoid telling people what they are *not*. We want to highlight who they *are*!

Speaking original design takes practice for it to become natural. At first, it might feel a bit contrived because you have not been trained to think and speak this way. You will no doubt be confronted with *withholding*. Withholding will show up in a shortage of words, that feeling that you are unable to voice the things you feel and know to be true. Two things must occur to break through this opposition:

1) take time to write down your spouse's original design, then
2) speak it out loud to him or her

Practice speaking original design *("You are.")* statements out loud and with conviction. Remember, a person does not need to have perfected, demonstrated, or ever operated in his or her original design for that design to be true. Don't wait until you "see it" or feel like it; start now!

4. Persist with unfailing love

Speaking the truth in love, growing up in Christ, and coming into the full stature of Christ (Eph. 4:15-16) are part of a lifelong pursuit that should be intentional, aggressive, and peaceable. That pursuit needs to be intentional and aggressive because it will be opposed. You will be mocked by self, the world, and the enemy. Persistence is the heart condition each of us must possess.

In this pursuit, I've learned that **I seek to have ZERO tolerance for TOLERANCE.** Tolerance is very often a false value in our society. I will not tolerate lies, deception, and rebellion having access to my spouse, family, or home.

1 Corinthians 13:4, 13

Love never gives up, never loses faith, is always hopeful, and endures through every circumstance. Love will last forever. There are three things that will endure—faith, hope, and love—and the greatest of these is love (emphasis added).

■ The Transactional Power of Speaking Truth

The heart of the Father moving through us is transactional. By transactional, I mean that by our words or actions implementing spiritual truth, something takes place in the heavenly realms that has natural world results. We've talked throughout this book about the transactional power of repentance and forgiveness. So it is with speaking the truth in love. There is real power in those words that come from the heart and character of God.

Building a marriage in alignment with God's design must include the marriage partners having—and expressing—Christ's heart for each other. We must speak out of that heart with no withholding. We must have a pure heart of love and speak from it. If that heart is not pure, there will be no power. And if the words are not spoken at all, there will also be no power.

Christ's heart + love + purity + spoken words = power

Colossians 3:12-17

Since God chose you to be the holy people whom he loves, you must clothe yourselves with tenderhearted mercy, kindness, humility, gentleness, and patience. You must make allowance for each other's faults and forgive the person who offends you. Remember, the Lord forgave you, so you must forgive others. And the most important piece of clothing you must wear is love. Love is what binds us all together in perfect harmony.

■ Breaking Withholding through Blessing

God designed marriage to be the most intimate, most open, and most honest of all relationships. Withholding stifles that intimacy, openness, and honesty. It stifles affection and tenderness. In short, withholding hits at the very heart of a joy-filled marriage. Withholding means the unwillingness or inability to share our true heart, hopes, dreams, and hurts. Withholding shuts people out and isolates us from others.

The key to breaking the power of withholding includes learning to speak words of love and blessing from the heart. Consider the following truths the Apostle Paul emphasized in training the early church:

Romans 12:9-10

Don't just pretend that you love others. Really love them. Hate what is wrong. Stand on the side of the good. Love each other with genuine affection, and take delight in honoring each other.

1 Corinthians 13:1-3

If I could speak in any language in heaven or on earth but didn't love others, I would only be making meaningless noise like a loud gong or a clanging cymbal. If I had the gift of prophecy, and if I knew all the mysteries of the future and knew everything about everything, but didn't love others, what good would I be? And if I had the gift of faith so that I could speak to a mountain and make it move, without love I would be no good to anybody. If I gave everything I have to the poor and even sacrificed my body, I could boast about it; but if I didn't love others, I would be of no value whatsoever.

The scheme of withholding takes a marriage out of alignment by:

- causing discouragement, rejection, and offense
- opening opportunities for the enemy to deceive and influence our spouse by creating a vacuum in which lies can be sown and believed
- stimulating perceived rejection and hurt feelings
- dampening a spouse's desire to please and serve
- creating an atmosphere that is emotionally and spiritually cold

Part of overcoming the scheme of withholding includes each partner in the marriage receiving a personal revelation of *God's love*. God's love is the most powerful, life-changing force in the world. If Satan can shut down people through withholding words of love, he can cripple God's Kingdom by paralyzing God's children and keeping them disconnected from Him and from one another. He also compromises a significant component of their original design, that of being priestly conduits of His power and blessing in their homes and communities.

When we freely bless, we release words of God's favor upon the people around us. The power of His Holy Spirit works through those words, as we operate in the authority of Jesus Christ. Jesus said, *"I will give you the keys of the kingdom of heaven; whatever you bind on earth will be bound in heaven, and whatever you loose on earth will be loosed in heaven"* (Mt. 16:19).

■ Blessing Your Spouse without Withholding

One of a man's most important jobs as gatekeeper in his home is to convince his wife that she is number one. That is, notwithstanding that the Lord is the Lord, when it comes to all else, she is number one! She occupies his desires and affections and attention and delight more than any other person, place, or thing.

In my experience, for the average man the above is true in his heart of hearts, BUT:

1. He has assumed (wrongly) that she knows it.
2. He doesn't know what it takes to convince her.
3. He doesn't know how to vulnerably and authentically speak truth from his heart.
4. He hasn't laid down his life for her.

Ephesians 5:25-31

Husbands, love your wives, just as Christ loved the church and gave himself up for her to make her holy, cleansing her by the washing with water through the word, and to present her to himself as a radiant church, without stain or wrinkle or any other blemish, but holy and blameless. In this same way, husbands ought to love their wives as their own bodies. He who loves his wife loves himself. After all, no one ever hated his own body, but he feeds and cares for it, just as Christ does the church—for we are members of his body. "For this reason a man will leave his father and mother and be united to his wife, and the two will become one flesh" (emphasis added).

My wife is at her best when she is secure in my love for her. That is God's design. My job is to love her sacrificially with everything: not only word, not only deed, but word, deed, heart, body, and soul. My job is to be completely honest, transparent, and open with my deepest hopes, dreams, and feelings. My job is to pour into my wife with all my heart, all the time.

The enemy has tricked us men into believing that vulnerability is weak. Feelings are weak. Transparency is weak. And as a result, all too often our wives starve for true love, the love of Christ demonstrated by their husbands.

For wives, many times where withholding comes into the picture is in the form of discontent and disengagement. In our work with couples, we often see women who are unsettled, quietly agitated at their circumstances, and stuck in what appears like depression. This often gets attributed to having young kids and being up a lot in the night, being discouraged by feeling stuck at home, or being overwhelmed by work pressures and responsibilities. Often these wives will pour into their kids or careers to the exclusion of their husbands. They may make demands for the husband to buy a bigger house, make more money, or change jobs. They are looking for security, believing the lie that they can look to circumstances, material things, or a sense of accomplishment for their affirmation and contentment. This perpetuates and reacts to the scheme of withholding. Many wives believe the love they feel (or don't feel) from their husbands is as good as it's going to get in the marriage, and they must look elsewhere for fulfillment. They stop building him up (and very often start tearing him down instead). Rather than being their husband's best friend, advocate, and cheerleader, they retreat to the sidelines or head in a completely different direction.

I've found that when a woman operates in this mindset, she disengages with more than just her words. She retreats emotionally and practically and so does the husband. It's kind of the classic question, "What came first, the chicken or the egg?" Did the wife start withholding first, or did the husband? Who is reacting to whom?

"He did."

"She did."

We can stand around pointing the finger all day and get nowhere—or we can, in faith, step out of the pattern of withholding and into God's design for speaking and living out the truth in love toward one another.

Kingdom marriages—marriages in alignment with God's design—intentionally and constantly speak words of life and love from the heart. They look for ways to bless each other. Once couples learn how to do this, I've found almost without fail that it brings their relationship into alignment with God's heart for communicating love and releasing His power and favor through their words. They find themselves able to integrate the heart posture of favor and blessing into their lives and operate in it seamlessly toward each other throughout the day.

■ Receiving the Truth in Love

We have mostly focused in this chapter on *delivering* the truth in love. But what about *receiving* the truth in love? Most of us can be quite prickly in our expectations of how people correct us. Our feelings are easily hurt and we quickly dismiss the correction given if it is not delivered perfectly. I am easily offended if someone is harsh or short or terse in their delivery of truth into my life.

But remember, once again, that in God's Kingdom everything is flipped upside down from the way the world socializes us. In God's Kingdom, we want *truth*. We *want* correction and revelation when we are not living in alignment with the truth. Humility is the quality of Jesus that sets us up for hearing the truth.

When humility becomes mature in us we begin to ask people to speak into our lives. When humility becomes mature in us we don't care *how* they speak it, we just care *that* they speak it and without hesitation. When humility becomes mature in us, we lay down our pride and reputation and illusions of perfection and just receive the truth as a gift from God—and from our spouse.

■ So Why Don't We?

David and Carly had been married 10 years. They had made a great life for themselves in their community. They volunteered countless hours to their church and were invested in their children's schools and activities serving in a number of capacities. They had wonderful friends and overall felt very blessed.

When juggling the daily demands of life, they worked very well as a team. They were excellent at communication when it involved work, parenting, house decisions, volunteer positions, vacations, and friends. Those were the easy topics. When it came to matters of the heart, however, the conversation was shut down.

For some time, David had observed areas of Carly's life that created challenges for the marriage or for Carly personally. He had tried to approach what they called the "hot topics" with no success. For them it was the topics of health, fitness, and money. When David did raise any of these topics, he was met with resistance. Carly believed that if anything needed to be addressed or changed, it was perfectly acceptable that it should be on her terms, in her timing. Over the years they developed the pattern of David raising a topic, Carly lashing out, and David fearfully retreating. David would stuff his feelings, concerns, and emotions until he couldn't control them any longer and then he would erupt. That wounded Carly and she would dig deeper into control and independence. They were stuck!

Fortunately for them they were living amongst a community of believers where they witnessed other couples who were able to speak truth in love to one another and maintain unity in the process. When they met with us, Carly was afraid. She had such a tight grip on certain areas of her life that just the thought of exposing them or letting go seemed too hard. She either did not want to change, was embarrassed that she was having a problem, or was afraid of what she would have to do to meet David's expectations. To her credit she laid her concerns and fears on the table for the four of us to look at.

The process of repentance and forgiveness was the starting point. Both needed to repent and forgive for years of dialogue that did not build the team. What happened in the weeks after that were discussions of the "how" to speak truth in love. They realized that they both "hear" truth in love differently. David doesn't need a lot of detail. Carly does. David does not need the truth "sandwiched"—he's all meat and prefers things be said as succinctly and directly as possible. He can hear it, receive it, and it inspires him to move forward with obedience. He had been using that style with Carly because that is what works for him.

To Carly, however, that style seemed cold, abrasive, and hurtful. David learned that more than the topic being discussed, Carly needed to hear his love and experience his tenderness during the conversation. When that finally started to happen, it paved the way for Carly's heart to open up and receive the blessing of David's eyes on her life and the freedom to engage in discussing the "hot topics."

In my experience, there are several lies that try to block us from speaking the truth in love to one another. By confronting these lies we can overcome the fears that keep us locked in patterns of withholding, tolerance, and mediocrity. Prayerfully and honestly consider the following list; are any of them in your game? Check any that apply.

Fear of reaction—
"If I speak the truth here . . ."
- ❏ S/he will just blow up.
- ❏ S/he will just shut down.
- ❏ S/he will keep score.
- ❏ S/he won't listen.
- ❏ S/he will just bring up all my shortcomings.

Fear of confrontation—
- ❏ I don't want to dwell on this all evening.
- ❏ I fear the history of how confrontation goes.
- ❏ It is just my deal and I need to become unoffendable.
- ❏ S/he really doesn't buy into the idea of original design anyway.
- ❏ I will only tell part of the deal.

Fear of counterattack—
- ❏ What about the log in my own eye?
- ❏ "You focus on yourself, I will focus on myself."
- ❏ "Get yourself fixed before you approach me."
- ❏ I will sugarcoat it.

Fear of withholding—
- ❏ It is going to be days or weeks before we can be intimate or affectionate.
- ❏ S/he is going to just shut down.
- ❏ S/he is going to pout.

❑ There will be a lack of peace between the two of us for who knows how long.

Fear of conflict—

❑ We have gone over this so many times, I think I will avoid the conflict.

❑ S/he has such a temper.

❑ I will just avoid this because we are not even close to being on the same page.

Fear of hurting the other—

❑ I don't want to criticize the one I love.

❑ I don't want my spouse to feel badly.

❑ I don't want him/her to think he/she is not doing a good job.

❑ I will say it in a way that makes it my fault.

Fear of losing control—

❑ I don't want my spouse to grow because it will make me look bad.

❑ I don't want him/her to advance more quickly than me.

❑ I need to get my leadership in line first and then I will speak.

❑ I sinned today; tomorrow when I am sin-free I will say something.

Check any of the above boxes that relate to you. With your spouse, pray through all areas where you have given access to fear to block speaking the truth in love. Use the 4R prayer outline to guide you: repent, rebuke, replace, receive. Go for spiritual transaction!

Here is where the desperation piece comes in. If we are truly desperate, we don't have anything to lose. Speaking the truth in love becomes a risk-it-all, full pedal-to-the-metal acceleration. We hold nothing back . . . we go for it!

■ Know What Discourages Your Spouse from Speaking Truth to You

I always ask spouses to learn to identify the things in themselves that make it difficult for the other person to speak truth, even in love. We all tend to use defensiveness, interrupting, blame-shifting, self-justification, the "silent treatment," and other mechanisms when we feel threatened, accused, or even "attacked," no matter how gentle the approach. We need to learn to lay down those self-protective practices and be genuinely vulnerable and approachable if we are going to reap the benefits of speaking from the heart with one another. We cannot make our spouse pay a cost to speak into our life.

I compare this tendency to make the other person "pay a cost" to what an octopus does to protect itself when threatened. The octopus has a defensive capability by which, when in danger, it expels an ink behind which it can hide in order to escape the current danger. As humans, we often use similar defense mechanisms to protect ourselves, especially as it relates to having truth spoken into our lives. Some are obvious to us while others we might not recognize.

These might include (but are certainly not limited to):[9]

❑ Time Demands: You simply are too busy for anyone to see what's really going on with you—too busy to listen to your spouse, to understand, to go deep.

❑ Disabling Circumstances: Things are so hard for you that it seems the only appropriate response to you is pity and help, not correction. You might even be offended that your spouse can't see how hard it is for you.

❑ Leadership/Responsibility: There is so much on your plate or your position is so important that others are intimidated. You might portray the "hero" image so others don't think they have a place to speak into your life.

❏ Troubled Past: You believe, portray to others, and/or communicate to people how far you have already come, and convince them that they should be satisfied with the changes you have made and the growth you have achieved. *"Don't you appreciate where I have come from? How can you put more on me?"*

❏ Prove It to Me: The person speaking finds themselves on the defensive, needing to present an air-tight case, like a prosecuting attorney who needs to prove conclusively that he sees something in your life (examples, dates, quotes, etc.).

❏ Confusion/Martyrdom: *"I'm really trying to understand what you are saying but I just don't see it."* You just don't believe you could be blind to something in your life that is visible to others, so it must not be there. You must be misunderstood.

❏ Accusation: You cannot simply take ownership of your sin without bringing up the issues of the person speaking into your life.

❏ Religiosity: You claim to have already had revelation of what the other person is speaking to, and point out how you have already dealt with it.

❏ Presenting Your Credentials: When confronted with something, you display your knowledge, contribution, and/or accomplishments to invalidate any shortcoming that might be pointed out which you need to address (especially as it relates to your marriage).

❏ False Humility: You are completely comfortable talking through what your spouse may bring to you, but there is no resultant change. You take a humble posture with your speech, but there is no conviction or repentance.

❏ Illness, Injury, or Physical Limitations: The person speaking feels that he or she cannot add to your burdens. You seem justified in all your actions by your pain or difficulty.

❏ Defeat: You take a specific word of correction and interpret it as a judgment of deficiency superimposed over your entire life. This communicates to those who speak to you that they have crushed you. The truth-speaker then struggles with guilt and takes on a responsibility to encourage you.

❏ Shame/Condemnation: You strive so hard to do everything right that it is crushing to hear any word of correction. The person speaking into your life fears how you will "beat yourself up" if he or she brings something to your attention.

❏ Pride/Superiority: You respond with such confidence that those who present themselves to you with a concern "feel stupid," and that they can't express themselves well enough.

These "octopus ink" reactions can be passive or aggressive, depending on our personality. Here are some other ways we make others pay a cost to speak into our lives:

Passive Ink
❏ Silence
❏ Victimization/emotional manipulation (communicates we have been deeply wounded, rather than edified)
❏ Isolation/run/withdrawal
❏ Avoidance (no eye contact)
❏ Body language
❏ A lot of time and energy required after the encounter (it takes a lot of time and effort to restore intimacy after speaking into your life)
❏ Withholding (diverse and many ways)
❏ Passive/aggressive response
❏ Shutting down emotionally while interacting relationally

Aggressive Ink

- ❏ Defensive posture
- ❏ Blame/deflecting
- ❏ Retribution
- ❏ Right for comeback/competition
- ❏ Cutting the other person off before he/she can finish
- ❏ Body language
- ❏ Denial
- ❏ Remaining obstinate until the person is deflated or defeated
- ❏ Anger
- ❏ Intimidation
- ❏ Justification of self vs. taking ownership
- ❏ Disqualifying the speaker from speaking into your life by pointing out his or her sin or weakness
- ❏ Confrontational in response

TIME TO DRIVE—Practical Application Exercise for Couples

The exercises for this chapter are two-fold and should be done simultaneously. You will need to practice speaking the truth in love from your heart to your spouse. You will need to identify (and repent of) any ways you have withheld or deflected truth-speaking, or made your spouse pay a cost to speak into your own life. Are you desperate? Let it show.

1. Speak original design to each other for one minute each every day— not just what you appreciate about each other, but the truth about who God designed each of you to be: *You are a leader. You are a woman of faith. You have a heart for the poor and oppressed. You are creative and make life fun.* Take turns going first.

2. Speak "how much" you love your husband/wife, "how much" you need him/her, "how much" you are thankful for him/her. Let your heart speak in tenderness, gentleness, kindness, favor, and humility.

3. With the husband going first, recognize before your spouse the "octopus ink" you use to protect or defend yourself when you feel "attacked." Ask if there are other forms of ink that you did not recognize.

4. Looking your spouse in the eyes, repent to your spouse, ask his/her forgiveness, and declare the opposite actions and behavior that you will live out by God's grace. Grant and receive forgiveness, one to the other.

5. After both husband and wife have gotten this far, stand together hand-in-hand as a symbol of unity, and rebuke the enemy and all lies that have infiltrated the marriage to compromise and/or destroy it. Then declare truth. Husbands take the lead!

6. Pray for a "Holy Spirit filling" in your marriage. Ask the Lord to fill each of you, and your marriage, to live in a divinely empowered and protected marriage. Then seek the Lord together in prayer. Listen together to the Holy Spirit. Ask Him to tell you how you look as a couple in God's eyes (words, mental pictures, Scriptures, impressions, etc.).

CHAPTER SEVEN

Getting *Me* Right!

We use God's mighty weapons, not mere worldly weapons,
to knock down the devil's strongholds.

2 CORINTHIANS 10:4

A high octane marriage is a spectacular ride that we take together, in unity. It requires each of us understanding, agreeing, and operating in our God-designed roles for a Kingdom marriage. In this chapter, we look deeply at each individual spouse and dig down to the roots of any bondage that imprisons us and keeps us from getting right in our marriage. It is important that I get *me* right with God in order to experience the fullness of life that God designed for my marriage.

People are somewhat like plants in this regard. Everyone knows, for example, that you can kill a tree by killing its roots. No matter how big the tree—its trunk, branches, or leaves—and no matter how vital it may look to the eyes, if the roots are diseased the tree will suffer and die. Conversely, there are many plants whose leaves and blossoms appear dead (and in fact do die off every year) but whose root systems live on underneath the ground and miraculously produce new leaves and flowers every year. Which tree is more alive—the tree that appears alive but is really dead, or the tree that may appear dead for a season that is really alive? The answer is not found in the appearances. The answer is found below the level of what can be seen with the naked eye. The root system is the key.

Our lives and marriages can be compared to a tree. There are visible components (leaves, flowers, and fruit) and invisible components (including the root system). The visible part of a tree will reflect the health of the root system. Similarly, our visible lives and marriages are symptomatic reflections of the conditions of the spiritual roots in our lives. God presents us with this analogy in Scripture:

Psalm 1

Oh, the joys of those who do not follow the advice of the wicked, or stand around with sinners, or join in with scoffers. But they delight in doing everything the LORD wants; day and night they think about his law. They are like trees planted along the riverbank, bearing fruit each season without fail. Their leaves never wither, and in all they do, they prosper. But this is not true of the wicked. They are like worthless chaff, scattered by the wind. They will be condemned at the time of judgment. Sinners will have no place among the godly. For the LORD watches over the path of the godly, but the path of the wicked leads to destruction (emphasis added).

Accordingly, if we are going to build a life-giving, fruit-producing tree, we must start with the root system. We looked in earlier chapters at the reality of the truth that we live in one world comprised of two realms—the natural and the spiritual. Those who choose to ignore the invisible spiritual realm, and continue to focus their efforts simply on what they can see in the natural realm, will be drawn to the symptoms (and so-called solutions) reflected by the visible portions of the "tree." Psychology and counseling aim at modifying the symptoms presented by visible patterns and behavior. Many techniques have been developed within these respective fields to address such issues. The limitation of these kinds of approaches, however, is that they are symptom-focused—that is to say, you do not fix a tree that is dead at its roots by cutting off the fruit or trimming the branches.

Consider this analogy with respect to a marriage. After modifying the visible symptoms of a broken marriage with communication techniques and encounter weekends, what do you have left? A trimmed tree that looks better temporarily, yet with a dying root system of hurt, anger, unforgiveness, injustice, oppression, and deception.

God's truth is designed to address the root system of your life, not just your marriage. Through spiritual transaction, God's power is able to bring real and permanent healing to the damaged roots that lie far below the surface and out of sight to the naked eye. God's perfect, healthy design is reflected in Psalm 1 on the previous page—a tree planted by rivers of living water sustaining the production of fruit year after year. That is God's design for marriage!

Getting *into* alignment with God's truth and design
requires that we identify and address the root issues
that are *out of* alignment with that design.

But before tackling the marriage, each partner must first address his or her individual spiritual root issues. When marriage partners are spiritually healthy, whole, and in alignment as individuals, there is a much better chance for success at getting into alignment as a couple.

■ Understanding Strongholds

Another word for a spiritual root that is out of alignment with God's design is "stronghold." A stronghold is a lie or behavior that is out of alignment with God's truth and design that—left unchecked—develops into a pervading mindset or behavior pattern. The Apostle Paul identified strongholds as *"arguments and pretensions that set (themselves) up against the knowledge of God"* (2 Cor. 3:5).

Strongholds are avenues of influence in our lives through which the enemy seeks to distort God's truth and original design. Fear, for example, can be (and often is) a stronghold. It is a pretentious thought raised up against God's truth. God's truth says, "Do not be afraid," and "Do not fear," hundreds of times throughout Scripture. Instead, God says "Have faith."

Examples of Strongholds

PASSIVE				AGGRESSIVE		
MATERIALISM	CONDEMNATION		R E J E C T I O N	COMPETITION	HOSTILITY / HATRED	
LUST	INSECURITY	SUICIDE		BETRAYAL	ARROGANCE	
INFERIORITY	SHAME		A B A N D O N M E N T	JEALOUSY	CONTROL	
	DEPRESSION	APATHY		STRIVING	MURDER	
VICTIMIZATION	SELF-HATRED / BODY IMAGE			BITTERNESS / RESENTMENT	CRITICAL SPIRIT	
	HOPELESSNESS	SELF-PITY		ANGER / RAGE	PRIDE / CONCEIT	
PASSIVITY	FEAR			FEAR	REBELLION	

Fear can be a stronghold, whereas faith is God's design. Fear is Satan's scheme to steal faith from us. Fear leads to death and faith leads to life. Strongholds imprison us; God's truth and design sets us free. Getting into alignment is the process of breaking the power of strongholds and replacing them with the truth of God's design. Fear is only one such potential issue. Many of the most commonly encountered stronghold issues are identified in the chart above.

Satan's stronghold construction begins with our thoughts. This is why Paul says that our transformation begins with renewing our mind:

Romans 12:2

Don't copy the behavior and customs of this world, but let God transform you into a new person by changing the way you think. Then you will know what God wants you to do, and you will know how good and pleasing and perfect his will really is.

■ How Strongholds Develop

It is by your thoughts that you make decisions; your decisions become actions which soon become your values in life. These values begin to define you and then become your lifestyle. Eventually, your thoughts and lifestyle can become out of alignment with God's truth. At that point you may find yourself in varying degrees of bondage as Satan builds his strongholds in your life through the places of jurisdiction you gave to him.[10]

In Ephesians 4:26-27, we see a little more clearly how this happens: "'*In your anger do not sin;' Do not let the sun go down while you are still angry, and do not give the devil a foothold.*" The word translated "foothold" (or sometimes "opportunity") in this passage is the Greek word *topos*. The clearest biblical usages of the word *topos* refer to a defined place—a *specific territory, area, or land*.[11] The word indicates a tangible spot or place in the same way that there was no *topos* for Mary and Joseph in the inn (Lk. 2:7), and that Jesus has gone to prepare a place or *topos* for us in heaven (Jn. 12:2-3).

Topos can also refer to a district, town, or dwelling-place. Our English word "topography" is related to this word. It can also be translated to communicate a place of jurisdiction, or a place in which one has gained rights. The implication of Ephesians 4:26-27 is that even though one belongs to God, where there is *topos*, Satan has gained a rightful or legal place to operate in a person's life because it has been granted to him. Over and over, the Scriptures warn us, we are to be diligent in keeping the enemy from gaining this kind of access to our lives.

1 Peter 5:7

Stay alert! Watch out for your great enemy, the devil. He prowls around like a roaring lion, looking for someone to devour.

Once we allow a *topos*—or "opportunity"—for the enemy in our lives through unconfessed sin, a cycle can easily develop into a spiral of deepened bondage and destructive behavior, as illustrated in the diagram on page 129. These cycles, or entrenched behavior patterns, are what we refer to as "strongholds." Left unchecked, they are devastating—to us and to our marriages.

■ Nuclear Reactions

If dealing with our own strongholds isn't hard enough . . . guess what happens when one spouse's stronghold pushes the button of the other spouse's stronghold? You guessed it. Nuclear reaction.

For example, a husband comes home from work and the house is a mess, the kids are in an uproar, and his wife is tired and needing to have some adult conversation. But the husband is angry and entitled, thinking to himself, "I worked hard all day. I just want to come home to a clean, peaceful house with my wife filled with joy and energy." As he thinks these thoughts, he begins to get angry. His anger turns to withholding and when he goes to greet his wife, she can see and feel his anger and disappointment in her before he says anything. She feels rejected and discouraged and begins to think to herself, "I have been working hard all day just to keep the kids fed, clothed, and happy. If only he could come home and help." She begins to get resentful and angry and that, too, leads to withholding. He grabs the paper and she starts to make dinner. Nothing is said. But you can slice the tension with a butter knife.

Here is an example of passive strongholds pushing the buttons of other passive strongholds. The husband in this example may have a stronghold comprised of entitlement, anger, and withholding. Those strongholds push the buttons of the wife's strongholds of rejection and discouragement, which also lead to withholding. Now there is a nuclear build-up of withholding going on this home. Over time, resentment and bitterness will accumulate until one or both explodes and elects "fight or flight." This pattern of anger/ rejection/ withholding/ bitterness/explosion will continue until those individual strongholds are addressed.

Sometimes recognizing destructive or unwanted patterns in our marriages can help us identify deeper stronghold issues that need to be addressed. It is also helpful because we can start to understand the ways our own strongholds "push the buttons" of our spouse, and vice versa. If we can recognize and understand these interactions, it helps us to avoid the schemes of the enemy that incite us to push each other's button and predictably cause those "nuclear reactions."

The great news is that we can be free from the power of strongholds. We can break the destructive nuclear reactions in our marriage by crushing the strongholds and establishing new patterns built upon the truth.

■ How We Break out of Strongholds

Do you remember the concept of "spiritual transaction" that I introduced earlier? I started out this book by saying that one of the things that sets this book apart from so many other approaches to marriage is getting to "spiritual transaction." A spiritual transaction is us doing our part and God doing His. When we are obedient to initiate something He has asked us to do, He responds by releasing His power and promises into our lives.

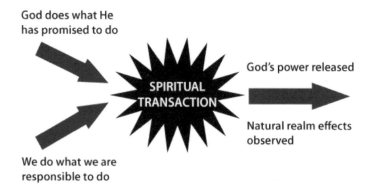

Simply put, we break out of strongholds by applying the power of the cross through repentance and then by exercising our authority in Christ to eradicate any bondage that may have resulted from our sin and choices. The result is freedom. Wherever there is genuine repentance and the exercise of authority and obedience, there is freedom. We cannot be free to start new patterns in our marriage until we are free from the core strongholds that have held us captive to past hurts, fears, injustices, and choices.

God's power through Christ is alive and well and available to us in real and tangible ways. It is especially available to us for the purpose of being set free from the power of sin as we come into alignment with God's original design.

Romans 8:1-2

So now there is no condemnation for those who belong to Christ Jesus. For the power of the life-giving Spirit has freed you through Christ Jesus from the power of sin that leads to death.

I believe this truth is just as real today as it was when it was written. Do you? If your answer is yes, then you must choose to live like it! Depend on it! Trust it! And experience it! You cannot afford to bury your head in the sand when it comes to sin. Everybody has sin. So deal with it—stop hiding and start hunting.

We want to *expose* our sin and strongholds so that we can be set free from them, so they can no longer influence our thoughts, control our behavior, and destroy our relationships.

That may require some work. The roots of our bondage are usually deep, and exposing them often requires some digging. The obvious or manifesting stronghold may not be the real issue; it might be merely the fruit. You and your spouse might need to seek the Lord together as to what the "root" really is. The real issue might be fear, wounds from an injustice, unforgiveness in another area, or perceived (or real) rejection or abandonment.

For example, someone may be exhibiting what looks like pride, competition, and workaholism. This behavior, however, is not the root; it is merely the fruit. A possible root is a childhood experience of rejection, abandonment, or poverty. The person is working himself (or herself) nearly to death trying to overcome a pervasive sense of worthlessness, fear, and/or lack of provision. The spouse reacts to the symptoms, "Why do you work so hard? We don't need the money. You don't care about me!" . . . but the real problem goes unnoticed—and unhealed.

Does that process sound intimidating? Don't be alarmed. Help is on the way.

■ Take Passivity and Control, for Example

In Chapter Three, we discussed the particular strongholds of passivity and control, and how they directly work against God's design for mutual brokenness, mutual submission, and mutual engagement. I'd like to revisit those strongholds here, because I find they are so foundational to helping couples walk out of destructive patterns in their relationship and into a place where they can most rapidly accelerate into God's design for their marriage.

When I am passive, Amy takes control. Somebody has to. Once she takes control, the effort required on my part to lead again often results in a tussle—and the thought or consequence of facing a tussle leads me to stay passive and let it go, avoid it, or work at cross-purposes—all of which lead to disunity. This is why the leadership of husbands is so key. When we don't lead, men, we open up a door to all kinds of problems.

This is not to say that men aren't controlling or that women aren't passive. Certainly that happens. But the overwhelming observation (and certain scheme of the enemy against God's design for marriage) is that passivity strikes at a man's design for leadership and control attacks a woman's design for faith.

Let's take a look now at how the strongholds of passivity and control may be affecting your marriage, and learn how to break out of them. Consider the following inventories and check all that apply:

■ Men: Passivity[12]

- ❏ I resist interdependence.
- ❏ I do not ask for help and I do not offer help / service to others.
- ❏ I see myself as more of a "private" Christian; I am reserved and keep to myself.
- ❏ I am critical of the way things are done in my church or job, and I have doubts about the leadership (I can see many flaws); it seems best for me to keep some distance and not get too involved.
- ❏ I tend to observe the activities of others (in family, socially, or in ministry); I rarely feel motivated or worthy to join in, or to initiate.
- ❏ I feel like I don't need anyone else.
- ❏ I resist obedience to the Lord by allowing sins to remain in my life.
- ❏ I do not seek the place of repentance.
- ❏ I have become familiar with, and indifferent toward, sins in my life.
- ❏ I do not believe it would do any good to take authority over sins in my life.
- ❏ I resist leadership because I don't want that much responsibility or pressure.
- ❏ I am familiar with feelings like fear and rejection, so I tend to believe that is the way things will always be for me.
- ❏ I am comfortable with the way I am.
- ❏ I allow myself to be comfortable with where I am spiritually. I'm fine with my walk with God right now.

❏ I allow myself to be comfortable with where I am emotionally. I have always struggled with (for example, depression, insecurity, shyness, fear, loneliness, etc.). This is the way things are, so why should I worry about it and try to find a "cure?"

❏ I allow myself to be comfortable with where I am physically. I don't care what others think of my appearance. Too bad if they don't like what they see.

❏ I often do what I want to do instead of what I ought to do.

❏ I tend to procrastinate household tasks, responsibilities, and obligations.

❏ I rarely initiate prayer or spiritual conversation with my wife.

❏ I allow my wife to make many of the decisions for our family because it takes the pressure off me.

Hebrews 6:11-12 NIV

We want each of you to show this same diligence to the very end, in order to make your hope sure. We do not want you to become lazy, but to imitate those who through faith and patience inherit what has been promised.

■ Women: Control[13]

❏ I think I am better at getting problems solved, and doing things correctly, than my husband.

❏ I have surrendered tasks like paying the bills to my husband, only to take them back again because of his (perceived) slowness, irresponsibility, or incompetence.

❏ I sometimes joke that my husband is like one of my children.

❏ I resist my husband's overtures of leadership, and find ways to assert my own will either overtly or passively.

❏ I determine if, and when, my husband and I will be intimate physically.

❏ I take other people's burdens upon myself and try to fix them.

❏ I sometimes act as my husband's or other people's Holy Spirit.

❏ My husband lets me make most of the decisions for our family.

❏ I try to persuade people to see things my way and take my advice.

❏ I notice and highlight other people's mistakes and shortcomings, in order to help them be better at what they do.

❏ I find myself telling other people how to do their jobs.

❏ I am critical and "put out" if my advice is not taken.

❏ I work hard to keep my husband on track, my children from making mistakes and getting hurt, and my friends healthy and happy. I feel responsible for them.

❏ When circumstances are out of my control, I sense something rising up inside me that wants to "take hold" of the situation and make it come out right.

❏ I sometimes use guilt, or emotional or spiritual pressure to make my husband conform to my will or ideas.

❏ I dislike anyone telling me what to do, or even *feeling* like I'm being told what to do.

❏ I am afraid that things would really fall apart if I didn't hold them together.

1 Peter 3:3-6 NIV

Your beauty should . . . be that of your inner self, the unfading beauty of a gentle and quiet spirit, which is of great worth in God's sight. For this is the way the holy women of the past who put their hope in God used to make themselves beautiful. They were submissive to their own husbands, like Sarah, who obeyed Abraham and called him her master. You are her daughters if you do what is right and do not give way to fear (emphasis added).

As you dive into this exercise, remind yourself that you want to "get *me* right." Affirm to yourself, "*I want to bring my original design into my marriage, not all of my strongholds and sin. I need help from my spouse to get free from the bondage I have been in. I want to take responsibility for my issues, for my past, for my sin, and for my strongholds. 'Getting me right' is one of the greatest gifts that I can bring into my marriage.*"

TIME TO DRIVE—Practical Application Exercise for Couples

■ 1. IDENTIFYING STRONGHOLDS

(For a detailed treatment of strongholds, I recommend *Living Free: Recovering God's Original Design for Your Life*, by Mike Riches, and the *Living Free Course*. Both are available from Sycamore Publications at www.sycamorecommission.org).

A. From the chart on page 128, identify what you believe are the five most prominent strongholds in your life. Write them down and add a one-phrase note as to how each might impact your marriage. For example:

Husband: *Passivity has kept me from leading my family and our marriage.*
Wife: *Fear has kept me from trusting my husband and encouraging his leadership.*

1. Show your spouse what you've written and ask if he or she thinks you have missed one, or if there is one unmentioned by you that impacts him or her.

2. Write down what he or she identifies. (Don't argue; just write it down. Remember what you learned about "octopus ink" in the last chapter.)

B. Helping your spouse through his/her stronghold and visa versa will require you partnering together:

1. Pray together before you begin. Be mindful of the one world-two realms principle. Ask for God's protection and invite the power of His Holy Spirit into your prayer time.

2. Helping yourself and your spouse ask questions is absolutely essential. You do not need to be the one with the answers. You can serve your spouse by helping him/her see what's going on. Some possible questions . . .

   ■ What are your emotions saying to you?
   ■ How are your emotions lying to you?
   ■ Where do you think you learned this?
   ■ How do you think you learned to act/respond this way?
   ■ What do you think the core lie is that you believe about yourself related to this stronghold(s)?
   ■ What do you think the core lie is that you believe about God related to this stronghold(s)?
   ■ What is the truth that combats the lie?
   ■ How would understanding (and appropriating) this truth affect the way you are acting?
   ■ How can I help you embrace this truth or how can I reinforce it in your life?
   ■ (DON'T USE THE "WHY" QUESTION)

NOTE: Working through a stronghold together will include a mixture of sharing together and working through issues together, but also going to the Lord together to listen to Him and receiving direction of the Holy Spirit through the Scriptures and Spirit-directed revelation.

■ II. PRAYING THROUGH STRONGHOLDS TOGETHER

A. If it is your stronghold that is being revealed, make sure that you invite your spouse to help you out of it and entrust yourselves to each other. Throughout and at the end your processes, pray together to accomplish spiritual transaction with God and one another about what has been revealed.

B. Go through each stronghold you identified together and apply the 4R's (transformational tools) to each—repent, rebuke, replace, receive (refer to page 41-42). Do the same for the items you checked on the passivity and control inventories.

C. You don't need to do all this in one sitting. Consider setting aside a "quiet time" each day for prayer and discussion, and tackle one stronghold each time. Try to identify the way your strongholds "play off" each other, and how you can be quick to recognize and dismantle that cycle when it happens. Help each other to be thorough and precise in dismantling the strongholds with the truth of Scripture and by declaring that you will operate in the opposite truth. This exercise will lay important groundwork for alignment in your marriage!

CHAPTER EIGHT

Becoming a Team

A person standing alone can be attacked and defeated,
but two can stand back-to-back and conquer.
Three are even better, for a triple-braided cord is not easily broken.

ECCLESIASTES 4:12

love the picture on the front of this book. There was a lot of discussion about whether or not to use it. I had to go all the way to Ducati of North America to get permission. I told them the picture was perfect for the marriage book I was writing and asked if they would grant me the rights to use it. They were excited about the project and readily gave me the necessary permissions to use it for the cover of my book. I was thrilled.

Why is it so perfect? First and foremost because it is a Ducati (just kidding). But seriously, can you see the teamwork in action? The couple is speeding down the mountain road, having the ride of their lives. Notice that he is leading. He is protecting. He is taking the wind resistance. They are one. Deeply connected.

She is right there with him, holding on, with both of their eyes focused simultaneously on the road ahead. They must work together in each of the turns in order to avoid a crash. The picture screams oneness, alignment, and team. Mostly it screams "fun and power, excitement and exhilaration." That's God's design for marriage! This couple is a dramatic and delightful picture of moving through life with force, freedom, and determination. They are completely synced up and doing life together. They are in alignment.

I've talked previously in this book about how the concept of alignment applies to marriage. One helpful definition of alignment is *the process of adjusting parts so they are in proper relative position*. Creating alignment in our lives and marriages is the process of adjusting components of our heart, mind, spirit, and patterns into proper position relative to the truth of God's design. This process takes transformation, and transformation comes from the power of God. We need God to help us experience this transformation. We cannot do it without Him. And by the way, He wants to help. In fact, He is waiting expectedly to help!

Isaiah 30:19 NIV

How gracious he will be when you cry for help! As soon as he hears, he will answer you.

As we have been learning and practicing, the first action step toward experiencing alignment in marriage is to enlist the help of the original Designer; that is, to get into alignment with the truth of God's original design. Remember how I also mentioned earlier the value of having every player on a sports team know his or her position and play it well? That's exactly the concept I'm talking about here.

Paul and Jennifer, for example, were a couple who thought they were doing just that—until they were confronted with the truth of God's original design for marriage and realized they were both energetically playing the wrong positions! They knew they needed help—God's help.

"We realize now," says Jennifer, "that we had an 'upside-down marriage.' The wrong person was calling way too many of the shots!"

From the outside looking in, Paul and Jennifer seemed perfectly happy. Paul was a highly relational guy who loved being a husband and father. Growing up as the youngest child of a large family, he was used to "going with the flow" and was quite content to let Jennifer make many of the decisions for their household. Jennifer, as an eldest child in her family of origin, had a capable, action-oriented personality and quite naturally gravitated to taking and delegating responsibility. It seemed a good fit, from a human perspective.

Paul and Jennifer had been married fifteen years when they became a part of a church that was teaching on the biblical principles of original design and God's plan for marriage. It was not long until they were confronted with some specific truths and promises from God's Word that they were unwittingly missing out on. It was a wake-up call for both of them.

"We were missing out on peace, primarily," admits Paul now. "Although Jennifer and I had very little overt conflict between us, I was resentful down deep. I knew there were areas of my relationship with Jennifer that were out of alignment—but I was afraid to admit it. I was afraid to take on the responsibility she seemed so capable of managing, for fear I'd fail. So I just went with it."

Jennifer agrees that peace was what was missing. "Although I generally felt capable of managing a lot of responsibility, I frequently felt overwhelmed and anxious—and resentful that Paul wasn't 'doing more.' I didn't realize that all he needed was for me to step aside and trust him—or rather, trust God to work through him."

Paul and Jennifer confessed these revelations to God and to each other, repenting of their respective fears, resentments, and coping mechanisms. They extended full forgiveness to one another and committed to living out God's design for their marriage, no matter how much work it would be to learn how. There was definitely a period of adjustment, they both admit. However, they are now confident and much more peace-filled in their relationship and roles. Jennifer has learned to trust Paul's judgment and decisions and not jump in so quickly if he doesn't act on her timetable. Paul has learned to be more firm and decisive, and to take initiative with household decisions and activities instead of waiting for Jennifer to pressure him before he acts. He is committed to initiating open communication and prayer with Jennifer and the kids, and actively monitors and directs the family's schedule and pace rather than just "going with the flow."

"If marriage can be compared to a game," says Paul, "it was like the Referee blew the whistle and called a foul on us. He took us out of the game for a 'time-out' and a re-reading of the play book. When we were willing to play in the positions we'd been assigned, He put us back in the game—and now we feel like we're playing as a winning team."

Jennifer adds with humor, "God took our upside-down marriage and turned it right-side-up!"

Be humble before God as you, too, confess your need for His help with your marriage. If you are reading this book as a couple, work through the exercises together with your spouse. If you are reading it by yourself, pray on your own and just be responsible for your own part at this point. Either way, invite the Lord into your process of making the necessary adjustments to bring yourself and your marriage into alignment with His original design.

Your next step will be to discover what that original design actually looks like in your own life and marriage. What are God's intentions and parameters for the institution of marriage? For the roles and responsibilities that each spouse is to fulfill? And for the particular style and manner in which you and your spouse will carry out these roles and responsibilities in your own home, according to *your* individual design(s)?

With that in mind, let's take a look at God's practical design and intentions for marriage, so we can make the necessary adjustments that will bring us, personally, into alignment with them.

■ God's Economy: Understanding Biblical Submission and Authority in Marriage

God's economy is a Kingdom. It is ruled by a King. He has thoughtfully designed a structure for His kingdom to ensure His protection and provision. It is a perfect design, intended to sustain Kingdom Life — and Kingdom Life is spectacular, as Jesus pointed out: "*I have come that they may have life, and have it to the full*" (Jn. 10:10, emphasis added). And because Jesus declared that giving us "life in all its fullness" was His purpose, that must be central to *our* purpose in everything we do — including (and especially) in our marriages.

God created and set up His economy — "Kingdom Life," we may call it — in the context of order and government (I am not referring to man-made political structures here, but rather to the process of "governing," which needs to occur within any human institution whether it be a country, a community, a family, or a marriage). God Himself lives within a governmental structure. God exists as a Trinity (Father, Son, and Holy Spirit), whose structure and relationships reflect the government of God. **God's "government," on a practical level, operates in alignment to established authority with mutual submission in the context of unity.**

It is important to understand that this structure is not a value statement. God the Father, God the Son, and God the Holy Spirit have equal value. However, they choose to live in submission to the established governmental structure, honoring one another without individual concern for diminishment in value.

As humans, God created us in His own image (Gen. 1:26-27). One aspect of this capacity to "be like God" is His design for us to live within the same relational order in which He lives. God himself functions in submission and authority within the Trinity, without submission or authority dictating value. God the Son submits to the Father and God the Spirit submits to the Son and the Father.

I bring up this point because I find that, very often, this truth elicits negative reactions when people hear the words "submission" and "authority." I believe those terms have received a bum rap over the years, especially as they relate to God's plan for marriage. God's design is never to bring diminishment, insignificance, or domination. As Jesus reminded us, His design is to bring LIFE—and life with fullness (Jn. 10:10). God's design for mutual submission and clear authority are part of what brings the fullness of Kingdom Life into our marriages and families.

The Apostle Paul illustrated God's Kingdom design for the operation of submission and authority in marriage as he was organizing the early church:

1 Corinthians 11:3

But I want you to understand that Christ is the head of every man, and the husband is the head of his wife, and God is the head of Christ.

Accordingly, with regard to *structure and authority* (not value), God's economy looks like this:

God

⇓

Christ

⇓

Husband

⇓

Wife

With regard to value, however, the Scriptures make it clear that God does not value males over females, or husbands over wives: *"There is neither Jew nor Greek, there is neither slave nor free man, there is neither male nor female; for you are all one in Christ Jesus"* (Gal. 3:28). He loves and values all of His children equally. But within that family of love and value, there is order and structure—and we need to get into alignment with it in order for our marriages and families to operate in the all fullness God intends for us to experience.

■ God's Marriage Team Structure

When Amy and I were first introduced to the biblical governmental structure for marriage, we were about twenty years old and in premarital counseling preparing for our wedding. Like most young couples, we were given a set of wedding vows to read and consider. When we saw the language "to love and obey," we just about choked. We immediately agreed that the word "obey" needed to be stricken because it did not reflect our heart for each other, or our belief in the equality of our value and roles in marriage. We have since learned that many couples in our generation felt similarly.

After over twenty years of marriage, however, both Amy and I now understand God's purpose and intention in His economy and authority structure. We now understand that *authority* is different than *value*. We now understand that authority does not have to be diminishing or abusive.

Let me say here that upon a first reading or shallow interpretation of the biblical passages describing God's design for marriage, some people are immediately turned off and shut down. Often this is because of a bad experience (or a lifetime of bad experiences) with authority. It's true that many mistakes and abuses have been committed in the name of authority, and many people have been hurt in relationships where they submitted to a person (or people) in authority. I suspect there will always be those who abuse their authority, which means there will always be those who are hurt by authority figures. That is not acceptable nor is it endorsed by Scripture or this book. But it also doesn't mean that we should throw out the truth because some have abused it for their own benefit.

When we talk about authority and submission, we're not condoning abuse or unhealthy relationships in any way. Rather, we're talking about God's children experiencing the fullness of joy and Kingdom Life that God intended for us. *God's design is not the problem. People are the problem!* God did not design anyone to be dominated by angry and hurtful authoritarians. People who have abused others with their authority have not operated in God's designed authority.

Those who have chosen to embrace the truth of *God's design* about authority and submission have found new life and joy in their marriages, families, and each area of life where these truths are applied.

My encouragement to you is to not let past hurts or offenses steal from you the truth of God's design, and the joy of Kingdom Life that will follow as you grow in alignment to the way God meant for you to live. I realize this is easier said than done and that past hurts are real. But bear with me and keep reading. We will engage in the truths and tools we have been learning and, as we align with them, God will bring healing to those past hurts and offer a path to freedom.

■ What Life-Giving Submission Looks Like

Contrary to some popular misinformation, submission is not a gender-exclusive quality. Scripture equally emphasizes that God designed us all to submit to *one another* and to the Lord (emphasis added):

Ephesians 5:21

(To husbands and wives) *And further, <u>submit to one another</u> out of reverence for Christ.*

Titus 3:1

Remind the believers to <u>submit to the government and its officers</u>. They should be obedient, always ready to do what is good.

1 Peter 2:13-14

<u>*Submit yourselves for the Lord's sake to every human institution*</u>, *whether to a king as the one in authority or to governors as sent by him . . .*

Hebrews 12:9

Since we respected our earthly fathers who disciplined us, shouldn't we <u>submit even more to the discipline of the Father</u> of our spirits, and live forever?

Hebrews 13:17

<u>*Obey your leaders and submit to them*</u>, *for they keep watch over your souls as those who will give an account.*

Jesus set the example for all of us when it comes to the ultimate expression of submission, as described by the Apostle Peter, *"He did not retaliate when he was insulted, nor threaten revenge when he suffered. He left his case in the hands of God, who always judges fairly"* (1 Pet. 2: 23). Here, Jesus was submitting to the religious leaders. He also submitted to the government (Mt. 17:27), to His own parents (Lk. 2:51), and to God the Father (Jn. 5:30). What does biblical submission look like? Bottom line: It looks like Jesus! And since (hopefully) all of us, as believers, are moving toward being conformed to the image of Jesus Christ (Rom. 8:29), submission is a character quality that we are all to be cultivating.

Specifically, though, within the context of the marriage relationship, Scripture tells us that God's design is for wives to submit to the authority of their husbands and for husbands to love, protect, and provide for their wives. God asks that His daughters submit to their husbands in the same way they submit to the Lord—and that His sons, at the same time, treat His daughters (their wives) as He would (1 Pet. 3:7)—with tenderness, compassion, and honor. Wives demonstrate their heart attitude towards the Lord by their submission quotient toward their husbands. Husbands should expect to give up their lives for their wives. These truths work together. However, neither is contingent upon the other. God looks to each of us to do our part regardless of whether our mate is doing his or hers.

Colossians 3:18-19

You wives must submit to your husbands, as is fitting for those who belong to the Lord. And you husbands must love your wives and never treat them harshly.

Ephesians 5:21, 25

And further, you will submit to one another out of reverence for Christ. You wives will submit to your husbands as you do to the Lord . . . And you husbands must love your wives with the same love Christ showed the church. He gave up his life for her . . .

1 Peter 3:1, 7

In the same way, you wives must accept the authority of your hus-
bands . . . In the same way, you husbands must give honor to your wives.
Treat her with understanding as you live together. She may be weaker
than you are, but she is your equal partner in God's gift of new life. If you
don't treat her as you should, your prayers will not be heard.

Why does God's word speak so strongly about authority, submission, and structure in the passages about God's design for marriage? Can we assume that it
is because He considers these truths important—and perhaps even foundational—to a high octane marriage? I believe so!

Amy and I would say that getting into alignment with God's authority
structure in our marriage was the most important change we ever made. This
process consisted of developing and cultivating a heart condition of mutual
submission, and a faith in God to help us live true to our roles in His design. It
took a step of faith that this "counterintuitive" truth would produce life-giving
results. It did. And it was big!

I began to learn that being the head of the family didn't just mean I got to
be "in charge." It meant I was to really love Amy selflessly, and lay down my life
for her. Amy began to learn that being my helper and manager didn't mean she
was my doormat or my servant. It meant she honored God by working in unity
with me, by being the one who effectively administrated many aspects of our
family and household life, and who brought nurture, life, and laughter to all of
us. Amy began to trust that God would lead me in leading our family and that
when she trusted me, she was ultimately trusting Him.

At the risk of sounding harsh, I would be remiss not to mention that to not
submit is sin—for all of us, to not submit to God, to not submit to our employers
and other government authorities. To not mutually submit to each other and

to not submit within our family—is sin. To appear to be submitted, but secretly in our heart or behind closed doors to be otherwise, is sin. So, too, with our spouse, if we are only pretending to submit and behind their back we are rebellious and disrespectful, we are out of alignment and opening spiritual doors to the enemy's jurisdiction.

To not submit is sin—for all of us.

Amy and I also learned that until we realigned our hearts and actions with God's design and sustained that alignment, God could not bless our marriage with the Kingdom Life of His design. But once we did, that was when we really began to see ignition in our marriage. That was also when we really began to see an exponential increase in the peace and joy and exhilaration quotients in our lives. That's where the rubber met the road!

■ Turning Into a Team

It's hard to get into alignment with something—to "submit" to it—if we don't know exactly what the standard is, isn't it? So one of the first steps in bringing a marriage into alignment is to seek understanding and clarity about God's design for marriage as the standard for experiencing LIFE as God intended. Then, we need to overlay our present situation and relationships against that standard in order to identify areas that are not in alignment. Once those areas are identified, we have some clear direction on where to focus our efforts in terms of transformation, both as a couple and as individuals.

Remember that real change or transformation requires the power of God. We appropriate that power through the work that Jesus did on the cross, giving us access to God's power through repentance and forgiveness. The power of the cross contains the power of LIFE. It was God's way of restoring LIFE to His creation. It is also His way of restoring LIFE to your marriage. Consider the truths below:

Romans 6: 6-7

Our old sinful selves were crucified with Christ so that sin might lose its power in our lives. We are no longer slaves to sin. For when we died with Christ we were set free from the power of sin.

Romans 8:2-4; 12-13

. . . the power of the life-giving Spirit has freed you through Christ Jesus from the power of sin that leads to death . . . God destroyed sin's control over us by giving his Son as a sacrifice for our sins. He did this so that the requirement of the law would be fully accomplished for us who no longer follow our sinful nature but instead follow the Spirit . . . So, dear brothers and sisters, you have no obligation whatsoever to do what your sinful nature urges you to do. For if you keep on following it, you will perish. But if through the power of the Holy Spirit you turn from it and its evil deeds, you will live.

Getting into alignment, simply put, means:

- understanding the plumb line of truth that God has designed for each of us (our original design)
- understanding where we are living outside of that design (our sin and strongholds)
- repenting and exercising our authority in Christ to overcome those sins and strongholds

- understanding the plumb line of truth that God has designed for marriage
- understanding where we as a couple are living outside of God's design for marriage
- repenting of where we have not been in alignment with God and one another
- forgiving one another

■ Nothing "in-between" Us

One more principle to consider as you are working toward agreement is to have "nothing in between you." The idea here is that whatever is standing in the way of agreement, you place out in front of you. We actually have couples sit next to each other on the couch and put an object on the table in front of them. The object symbolizes the point of disagreement. Now the couple is sitting next to each other like a team and together they face the opposition (the object on the table). So, for example, if we are having trouble agreeing on how to handle finances, we put all of the issues regarding the finances out in front of us and we sit next to each other symbolizing that we are a team. We are going to attack the issue of finances together.

**We are going to be more *for the team*
than we are *for ourselves*.**

Imagine taking an object symbolizing your area of disagreement and placing it between you. Now, to address the issue you turn toward each other with the object (or issue) in between you. Sometimes, in order to emphasize the point, I ask couples to hold their hands as if they are pistols and point them toward the object sitting between them. Then I ask, "What is going to happen when you both start firing your pistols at the object?"

The inevitable answer always comes. "We are going to hit each other." That, of course, is what always happens when we allow issues "in between us."

When we allow any issue in between us, we are essentially saying that the issue is more important than our team, more important than our unity. Can I just say that there is no issue that we face as couples that is more important than preserving and fighting for our unity?

■ Assessing Alignment

We looked at individual transformation for marriage partners in the last chapter. In the present chapter, we want to experience the revelation and spiritual transaction necessary to bring transformation to the marriage *team*. In addition to our individual design, God has also given *marriage* an original design and we need to apply the same perspective to our marriage. We need to ask ourselves these questions:

1. What is the truth? (the original design of marriage)
2. Where does our marriage line up in honest comparison with that truth? (evaluation, revelation)
3. What must we do to get into alignment? (repentance, forgiveness, authority)

Throughout this book, you have been—and will continue to be—invited to engage in exercises of spiritual transaction that include repentance, forgiveness, and exercising spiritual authority. It is precisely this work that will bring transformation and alignment to our lives, marriages, and families—and ultimately to our churches, communities, and nations.

Where you and your spouse recognize you have not been living in alignment with God's original design for marriage, you now know you can repent—to the Lord and to each other. Forgive one another for past mistakes, failures, miscommunications, and disappointments. You can use the evaluation questions listed on the next pages to help prompt your thoughts, conversations, and prayers.

The questions that follow will generate conversation around God's design for marriage and where your marriage is in relationship to that design. Talk through these questions in preparation for the exercises at the end of this chapter. With respect to each topic area, ask yourselves, "Is there unity on this topic?" "Do we agree about our goals and methods for doing life together?" If these questions expose areas of disunity or disagreement or past hurts and failures, you now know how to deal with that—repent, forgive, and develop a plan that you both agree on.

■ Questions for Husbands

Who handles the finances?

Are finances in order, working, and is there agreement?

Specifically, what does that look like?

Is everyone at peace and excited about how that is working?

Who disciplines the kids?

Are there private conversations about how you discipline? Who explains it to the kids?

Do the kids always see unity in their parents?

Do you always feel like a united team when dealing with issues with the kids?

Is there confidence in dealing with the kids' discipline and training issues?

Is the husband leading in the spiritual development of family?

Is he asking the hard questions and praying and encouraging and showing the truths of Scripture?

Is he giving assignments and practical truths for further development and discipleship?

Is he praying over the family?

Is he providing protection?

Is the husband *carrying the burden* of provision, protection, discipline, spiritual growth?

Is the husband initiating a heart of love for his wife and kids, and pouring out his heart to them?

Does the husband see the family as "his little flock?"

Is the husband demonstratively affectionate toward each family member?

■ **Questions for Wives**

Are you generally excited about respecting your husband at all times?

Do you have a heart that is full of respect?

How often do you tell your husband that you respect his leadership?

How often are you encouraging him to operate in more authority?

Are you stepping out of the way to allow him the opportunity to lead?

Are you stepping back with total encouragement for him to lead?

Do you interrupt him? (leading, talking, etc.)

Do you talk about your husband to others? (except emergencies)

Do you pray for your husband?

Do you have a gentle and quiet spirit?

Do your thoughts reflect the truth of who your husband is created to be?

Do you see yourself as his partner?

Do you know your respective role on the team?

Are you creating an atmosphere of peace, joy, and order at home and enjoying it?

TIME TO DRIVE—Practical Application Exercise for Couples

■ Alignment Assessment

Each of the following points represents an aspect of God's design for marriage. For each point, husband and wife should each assess whether the role is being fulfilled by the person to which it applies. Check the box if the other person is operating in your understanding of God's design. If your expectation and understanding of God's design is not being met, circle the box for further work and discussion. If either spouse doesn't check the box, immediately dig in with thorough repentance and forgiveness.

■ God's Design for Husbands: GATEKEEPER

- ❑ carrying the burden of provision and protection
- ❑ covering the family in prayer, spiritual warfare, safety, and provision
- ❑ policies in place for how family is to operate in the world (not running alone, not walking to cars alone at night, curfews, etc.)
- ❑ taking responsibility for the safety and welfare of the family (house rules)
- ❑ knowing your wife's friends and whether they build her up or tear her down
- ❑ knowing your wife's schedule and whether it brings life or sucks life out of her
- ❑ knowing your kids' friends and schedules and whether they are a positive or negative influence
- ❑ spiritual leadership, discipling wife, partnering with wife to disciple kids
- ❑ initiating parenting and partnering
- ❑ putting marriage first before self, work, kids, or ministry
- ❑ leading praying together
- ❑ being decisive and intentional

❑ sustaining all of the above for the long-haul

❑ sacrificial, giving everything up for wife and family

❑ making sure home is in order before committing to other things

❑ insisting on agreement in all things

❑ going first, leading in personal sanctification, devotion, discipline, integrity, love, sacrifice, service, purity, etc.

❑ relating to wife in an understanding way

■ God's Design for Wives: HELPER

❑ trusting the Lord by sustaining a submitted heart to husband, regardless of husband's condition or leadership

❑ respecting and honoring husband to his face

❑ respect and honoring husband to family

❑ respect and honoring husband to friends and community

❑ never talking negatively to anybody about her husband

❑ being "for" her husband

❑ creating and maintaining a peaceful, orderly home

❑ discipling kids

❑ putting marriage first before self, kids, work, or ministry

❑ making sure home is in order before committing to other things

❑ partnering with husband in such a way that he feels fully supported in his role and responsibilities

❑ trustworthy in handling the family's resources and schedule

❑ implementing agreed-on policies and procedures for family safety and standards

❑ operating in a gentle and quiet spirit

❑ seeing to needs of husband and family in advance

❑ experiencing life and joy in all of the above

■ Alignment Plan

Now that you have done the initial transactional work, the authenticity of your repentance will include action. Put a plan together for each of the issues where there has been disunity or disagreement. Start by asking the question, "What do I want [e.g. our parenting] to look like?" Try to start with the objectives you each want to reach.

Often times we are much closer to agreeing on objectives than we are on *how* to get there. However, once we realize we both want the same thing, there is a much more cooperative spirit when discussing how to get there. For example, both spouses usually agree that they want to raise godly, capable, respectful, obedient, joyful children. But we spend so much time arguing about the best way to parent (or, more accurately, about how *my way is* the best way to parent), that we fail to realize we are in complete agreement about the goals and objectives about our parenting.

So start by establishing goals and objectives for each topic where there has not been unity. Then begin the process of developing a plan for how to achieve those goals and objectives. Don't get discouraged and don't ever give up or quit. Stay at the table of discussion until you each have a deep understanding of each other's heart about what is important on that topic. Where there is understanding of each other's heart, the possibility for agreement increases exponentially.

1. Discuss and write down your agreed plan for operating in alignment.

2. In prayer, put your list forward before the Lord and ask Him to speak to you about anything He would have you add, delete, emphasize, or clarify. Add these components to your list.

3. Identify which spouse is responsible for which components of your plan. Commit to pray for each and support one another in executing your plan. Make a date to check back in with each other soon and discuss how you're doing. Then run forward with your plan immediately!

SECTION THREE

Designed
for Exhilaration

C ongratulations! If you're reading this page you have made it through
Sections One and Two. You have learned about—and hopefully are
experiencing—the release of God's power in your life and marriage
through the truths (and application of the truths) in those chapters. If you are
not experiencing breakthrough, you may want to consider a few things.

Amy and I have never seen a couple combine the application of the truths
in this book (ancient truths from Scripture) and the heart condition of desperation, humility, brokenness, submission, and engagement and *not* witnessed a
transformed life and marriage. Therefore—if I can be so bold—I really believe
that if you are not experiencing the beginnings of the power of God's design
and the freedom that comes from getting in alignment with God's truth, then
there is possibly a heart condition issue. It is never God's truth that is the problem. It is usually us.

So if that's the case with you, I encourage you to take a few minutes for a
"heart check." Ask the Holy Spirit to speak to you about *you*. Then ask Him to

speak to you about your spouse and your marriage, to show them to you through *His* eyes, and to teach you how to really apply and live out the principles of a high octane marriage.

Next up: Section Three is essentially composed of practical truths to help you and your spouse overcome old patterns and sin reactions you have accumulated over the course of your life and marriage. I've called this section "Designed for Exhilaration" because of our experience with couples when they break free from the past and start charting a new course toward their future. They become excited and their faces light up. They are new people.

Many of us get tangled up in negative reactions and sin cycles and then get stuck in those patterns, which breeds hopelessness. Sometimes in that condition we are like discouraged motorists who have broken down on the side of the highway, with no progress made after excruciating effort. But help IS in sight. In these chapters we will embrace and experience the power of the truths of Hope, Faith, and Light. These truths will help us break out of hopelessness from past patterns and into the exhilaration of a bright and glorious future—a high octane ride marked by unity, joy, and excitement!

CHAPTER NINE

Hope vs. History

So be strong and take courage,
all you who put your hope in the LORD!

PSALM 31:24

Hope:

1. to wish for something with expectation of its fulfillment
2. to have confidence; trust[14]

W e've tried all this before. We've been to counseling but nothing has changed. We do well for a couple of weeks and then all the old patterns come right back and we're fighting again. I can't live like this anymore. There is no use even trying when there is not the slightest hope for real, lasting change."

"I just don't have the energy to try anymore. I can't risk the disappointment of failing again or worse—the disappointment of another of my spouse's failures. It would be easier just to split and start over."

Amy and I have listened to similar variations of the above accounts from at least half of the couples we've worked with. Hopelessness, unfortunately, is pervasive and can be fatal. It is also an absolute scheme of deception formulated by the enemy to destroy faith and expectation.

As we have counseled marriages through the years, one of the most common barriers to breakthrough we've found is the all-too-common tendency for people to define their marriage by past patterns and historical events. From the sheer number of encounters with this issue, I have to believe that this pattern is more than just a coincidence. Mindful of the "one-world-two-realms" principle, I am convinced there is a spiritual force at work to energize this mentality. I am convinced it is the work of the enemy to keep marriages locked down and prevent them from moving forward.

Are *you* hopeless? Do you ever catch yourself saying things like:

"He will never change."

"What's the use?"

"You always . . ."

"She never . . ."

These phrases are indicators of believing the lie of hopelessness, and entertaining these lies will compromise any relationship. Along with hopelessness, other emotions like defeat, disappointment, and discouragement enter in and rattle the very foundation of a marriage, undermining everything that has been built upon it. Sustained hopelessness effectively pulls a marriage completely out of alignment with God's design and truth for it, and leaves it there.

Hope, on the other hand, believes that:

"God will prevail."

"She will win."
"He will change."
"God is in charge."

1 Timothy 4:10

. . . our hope is in the living God, who is the Savior of all people, and particularly of those who believe.

Hope is based not on what is seen, but on God.

Jesus does not need to prove Himself again to us. His love is established for all time; He has not taken it back. His care for those who love Him is a sure foundation upon which we can place all our hope—and wisely so. When our hope is based on *Christ* as our sure foundation—rather than on a spouse or on the marriage itself—the winds of trials and circumstances, hurts and disappointments, or failures and injustices cannot shake it. Hope keeps us in alignment with God's love, truth, and perspective.

In Christ, there can be no question that our HOPE is grounded upon the firmest rock in all creation. There is no basis for doubt, no basis for losing heart, and no basis for fear. No matter what our eyes may see or our hearts may feel— we do not need to let hope fade or die. And through the power of God's Holy Spirit in our hearts, there is an endless supply of it for those who will reach out and take hold of it:

Romans 5:5

And hope does not disappoint us, because God has poured out his love into our hearts by the Holy Spirit, whom he has given us.

Picture it like this: Imagine a little boat carrying you and your spouse out on the ocean in the midst of the waves and swells. Millions of little splashes put water in your boat, which is slowly filling up. Discouragement sets in as you can see that your little boat has no chance against the force of the pattern of the water, waves, and swells relentlessly trying to sink your boat. Fear, urgency, anger, and division set in.

Now picture one of you shooting an arrow up into the sky. The arrow—which has a rope attached to it and your boat—lands on an aircraft carrier, which ties up the boat and makes it impossible for it to sink. Now you enjoy the wild ride, the waves, and the swells without fear—discouragement is forever crushed.

This is a picture of hope. Each marriage is like a little boat on the ocean of life, an ocean that will bring great opposition to the smooth sailing of our little boat. The forces opposing our marriages are overwhelming and relentless. But the aircraft carrier is not threatened by the waves and swells. It is trustworthy and tireless.

Hope is our personal agreement to tie up to the Lord, rest in His promise and strength, and enjoy the ride. NO MATTER WHAT!

Consider carefully each of the Bible passages about HOPE below. Read them slowly. Think about them. Declare them over your own life and marriage. If the lie of hopelessness surfaces in your thoughts as you do this, take those thoughts captive and make them obedient to God's truth (2 Cor. 10:5). Confess believing the lie of hopelessness. Rebuke the lies of the enemy and send them packing! Allow hope to grow in your heart, and let it bring your marriage back into the light of God's truth, the joy of Kingdom life, and alignment with His original design. The following verses will help re-align your thoughts (emphasis added):

Hebrews 10:23-24

Without wavering, let us hold tightly to the hope we say we have, for God can be trusted to keep his promise. Think of ways to encourage one another to outbursts of love and good deeds.

Psalm 33:20-22

We put our hope in the LORD. *He is our help and our shield. In him our hearts rejoice, for we trust in his holy name. Let your unfailing love surround us,* LORD, *for our hope is in you alone."*

Psalm 39:7

And so, Lord, where do I put my hope? My only hope is in you.

Psalm 43:5

Why am I discouraged? Why so sad? I will put my hope in God! I will praise him again—my Savior and my God.

Psalm 71:4-6

My God, rescue me from the power of the wicked, from the clutches of cruel oppressors. O Lord, you alone are my hope. I've trusted you, O LORD, *from childhood. Yes, you have been with me from birth; from my mother's womb you have cared for me. No wonder I am always praising you!*

Psalm 71:14-15

But *I will keep on hoping for you to help me*; *I will praise you more and more. I will tell everyone about your righteousness All day long I will proclaim your saving power, for I am overwhelmed by how much you have done for me.*

Psalm 78:7-8

So *each generation can set its hope anew on God, remembering his glorious miracles and obeying his commands. Then they will not be like their ancestors—stubborn, rebellious, and unfaithful, refusing to give their hearts to God.*

Psalm 119:49-50

Remember your promise to me, for it is my only hope. Your promise revives me; it comforts me in all my troubles.

Psalm 147:7-11

Sing out your thanks to the LORD; sing praises to our God, accompanied by harps. He covers the heavens with clouds, provides rain for the earth, and makes the green grass grow in mountain pastures. He feeds the wild animals, and the young ravens cry to him for food. The strength of a horse does not impress him; how puny in his sight is the strength of a man. Rather, the LORD's delight is in those who honor him, those who put their hope in his unfailing love.

Biblical hope is unwavering confidence in the person and promise of Jesus Christ, and in the unfailing character of God. The person who is marked by hope lives by the following creed:

THERE IS *ALWAYS* HOPE.
HOPE IS *ALWAYS* ALIVE.
JESUS WILL NOT DISAPPOINT, *EVER.*
HOPE ENDURES NO MATTER WHAT LIFE MAY BRING.

■ Hope is Agreement against the Lies of Patterns and History

Often the lie of hopelessness comes packaged in phraseology such as "People never change," or "You can't teach an old dog new tricks." Nothing could be further from the truth. God created everyone and He can recreate them (change them) any time He sees fit. Moreover, He has given us the tools we need to effect change in ourselves and in our marriages—divinely powerful weapons to counter the enemy's lies, take them captive, and make them subject to the truth of God (2 Cor. 10:3-5).

Hope does not allow past mistakes, failures, and patterns to steal the future of LIFE and joy in God's design. Hope looks toward a future of increasing restoration, healing, and unity.

Hebrews 6:11-12

Our great desire is that you will keep right on loving others as long as life lasts, in order to make certain that what you hope for will come true. Then you will not become spiritually dull and indifferent. Instead, you will follow the example of those who are going to inherit God's promises because of their faith and patience (emphasis added).

■ Hope Clings to Truth, not Performance

When truth is spoken (silently or aloud) it produces hope, like a "forget-me-not" plant. Where a forget-me-not is planted it grows and spreads like a wild fire. Hope sounds like:

"We're gonna get there!"

"The Lord is working."

"You're going to win."

"You are a leader."

"You are the head of this family."

"You are a patient mom."

In the process of building a high octane marriage, hope does not look to your mate. It does not look to present circumstances; it does not look to progress; it does not look to promises made by the other; it does not even look to positive changes as its basis. As I say this, I cannot help but think of the old hymn, "My hope is built on nothing less than Jesus' blood and righteousness."[15] Our hope is secure in Christ alone (1 Tim. 1:1)!

What is YOUR confidence in? Where do you place it? Are there areas in your marriage where God is giving you the opportunity to forge hope? Are there patterns and history of disappointments or habits that are destructive to the marriage where hope has been lost? If so, you're not alone. But take heart. There really is hope, as many have found.

When Frank and Sheila came to Amy and me for help with their marriage, Sheila's trust level was less than zero. Frank had failed catastrophically over and over again: Unfaithfulness, passivity, anger, remorse, shame, guilt, promises, and . . . the cycle would repeat over and over again. Already she had endured twenty years of broken promises without even the hint of change. She was done. Completely hopeless. She hung on for the kids' sake and out of fear of divorce.

As Sheila worked through the principles of alignment, forgiveness, and restored hope, she received a revelation of biblical hope. That hope was not based on promises kept or the performance of her husband. For the first time, Sheila learned that hope meant fixing her eyes on Jesus Christ, and Him alone.

She began to obey the truth of hope. She began to turn to Jesus for her hope. She renounced her own coping mechanisms and began to embrace (and live out) the truths of her own original design—both for herself personally and for her role in her marriage. She began to pray for her husband and trust *the Holy Spirit* to bring the conviction, change, and healing, rather than her own efforts and schemes.

Today, Frank and Sheila's marriage is transformed. Through repentance, forgiveness, obedience and consistently applied truth and hope, Frank was able to break free of old habits. Sin patterns are broken, and he has replaced them with alignment with God's truth and design for marriage. Today he is the leader of his family, in every sense of the word.

What would have happened if Sheila had given up hope when she wanted to? What if Frank had given up hope that things could ever be different? Thankfully, both of them laid hold of the hope that had been poured out in their hearts through God's Holy Spirit, and received the power to be transformed.

How do YOU want to live? Negative? Giving up? Down in the dumps? "Poor me?" Hope requires a fundamental choice about how we approach the life God has given us to lead.

Hope requires a fundamental choice about how we approach the life God has given us to lead.

Yes, lead. There is a lot packed into the concept of "leading your life." The critical difference in the HOPE of believers is in the One in whom we hope—Jesus Christ!

■ Hope is Agreement on Original Design not History

For hope to prevail, both spouses must agree that they will each defend the other person's original design against the lie of history and patterns. Hope is a catalyst for breaking those patterns. Hope smashes the "s/he will never change" curse.

Many years ago Amy and I, and our daughters, received prayer for our original designs. We kept the notes from those prophetic prayer times, typed them up, and hung them on our bathroom mirror. Today, they are a little spattered and worn. But they serve as a daily reminder to both Amy and me of who we really are. There are days when I need that reminder about who Amy is, when I am tempted to be discouraged by the trials and circumstances that any marriage encounters in this fallen world. And I know there are plenty of days when Amy needs that reminder about me. Invariably, we let each other down, and fail to live up to who God designed us to be. But our hope is restored and sustained when we keep our eyes on Jesus and on God's original design for our marriage and for us as individuals, and NOT on our daily circumstances and failures.

■ Overcoming Hopelessness from Patterns of Wounding

Overcoming hopelessness through faith in Jesus Christ is more than just picking yourself up by your bootstraps. It is more than the power of positive thinking. It's not just ignoring the problems in life that have contributed to the hopelessness. **Overcoming hopelessness through Christ is a tangible spiritual transaction that applies the truth of God's love, combined with the biblical principles of repentance and forgiveness, to our root hurts and disappointments.**

Many times the roots of hopelessness are wounds we have experienced early in life. Some of us have experienced hurtful words, abuse, accidents, or circumstances that are painful or lead to feelings of abandonment or anger. In response to those woundings we often react either passively or aggressively to the injustice. Our reactions, when outside of God's truth, often develop into patterns of self-protection. These patterns of protection lead to isolation and disengagement and buried anger on the passive side (self-hatred), or anger, wounding of others, or self-indulgence (self-centeredness) on the aggressive side. (Refer back to the stronghold chart on page 128 for a closer look at how love deficits and injustices (like rejection and abandonment) result in patterns of sin reactions that turn into ingrained strongholds and sin patterns in our lives.)

More subtle masking of wounding can be seen in issues of control. Fear of being hurt again leads to the need for a controlled environment where there is little risk of being hurt. Because the foundation of the system is fear, a controlled house is a house built on sand, which will not stand against the storms (Mt. 7:25-27).

Jesus' response to injustice and wounding was not hopelessness, but rather forgiveness. *"Father, forgive them for they know not what they are doing"*(Lk. 23:34.) Rather than respond out of His own emotions, He chose to entrust Himself to the Father: *"When they hurled their insults at him, he did not retaliate; when he suffered, he made no threats. Instead, he entrusted himself to him who judges justly"* (1 Pet. 2:23). This kind of forgiveness is the heart of the power of the cross.

Forgiveness is the key to unlocking the door to healing and restoring hope.

This is what Mary discovered. Her father had long since passed away but her pain and anger and fear from her father's abuse was very much alive. By the time she was a middle-aged adult, she was struggling to have any relationships, hold a job, leave the house, or even go on living. A friend of mine found her in a daze on the street.

In talking with her, my friend was struck with an overwhelming sense from the Lord that this woman needed to forgive her father. He asked her about her story, and listened as she lashed out at her father and told of horrific abuses that had left her in shambles and bondage with no way out. After all, her father had showed no remorse; she could not confront him and make him feel her pain. She felt stuck with no way out—hopeless.

Equally struck with the overwhelming sense that this would be an impossible ask of anyone, my friend struggled to say the words he knew would set her free. He recognized that what Mary was describing was the lie of unforgiveness, and entirely inconsistent with God's economy. So he bravely told her, "I think you need to forgive your father."

Mary was dumbfounded. This was not the sympathetic response she was looking for. She responded, "I can't." So my friend proceeded to explain that she did have a choice and that obedience in forgiveness would lead to healing and new life. In the following minutes she mustered up the courage to say those powerful words, "I forgive my father."

Today, Mary is happily married, healthy, and free. She has been absolutely restored through the power of forgiveness and faith in the work of Jesus Christ.

What wounds have a stranglehold on *you*? With Mary's story in mind, are there areas in your own life that keep you locked down in hopelessness and unable to move forward in the Life and freedom that God has for you? Perhaps your story is just as dramatic as Mary's. Or perhaps the injustices and disappointments you've suffered seem inconsequential in comparison. Either way, those wounds CAN be healed by the power of the cross and released through the granting of forgiveness.

Past hurts and injustices do not need to shut down you or your marriage. The first keys to freedom are—as we have been maintaining all along—repentance and forgiveness. We repent of our sin responses to other people's offenses against us. We receive God's forgiveness, then turn around and extend that forgiveness to others. The result: Pure freedom and a kick-it-into-high-gear release of high octane power for you and your marriage!

TIME TO DRIVE—Practical Application Exercise for Couples

■ Experiencing God's Design: Overcoming Wounding

This is an exercise in radical obedient forgiveness. The question isn't simply "Are you ready to forgive?" The question is "Are you ready to be free from all wounds and injustices?" and then, "Are you ready to obey?" This is usually a very powerful and transformational exercise. It is important to go through it together as husband and wife with compassion, encouragement, and support.

1. Put each unhealed wound or injustice on the table.
   a. Ask the question (of yourself and of the Lord), "Against whom am I carrying any unforgiveness?" Consider:

      i. Each of your parents
      ii. Children
      iii. Teachers, coaches, friends
      iv. Husband/wife
      v. Other injustices (circumstances)

   b. Write these down (make a list for each of you)

2. For each wound or injustice, declare forgiveness in prayer for the person who wounded you. For wounds between husband and wife, the offender should run to thorough and genuine repentance, and the

wounded party to obedient and permanent forgiveness. If the offender will not repent, the wounded party can and should still forgive.

Example:
Husband: *My father humiliated me in front of my friends when I was young and it has stuck with me all these years.*

The following can and should be proclaimed whether the husband's father is presently alive or not. If the Holy Spirit so directs, the husband could go to his father and forgive him in person. But this is not necessary for the spiritual transaction and freedom to get started in the husband's own heart.

> *"I forgive my father for every time he humiliated me in front of my friends. I forgive him for the way that made me feel, and for the pain and insecurity I have felt since that time. My dad is completely forgiven."*

3. After completing the above, in prayer before your spouse and to the Lord declare forgiveness and blessing over each and every person who has wounded you.

> *"Father, I ask Your forgiveness for my sin of unforgiveness toward my father all these years. I receive Your forgiveness and in obedience and conviction, I declare that forgiveness toward my dad for humiliating me is complete. I bless my dad with all my heart and with the fullness of life and joy."*

4. Identify the ways these past hurts and injustices have affected you and your spouse with regard to your relationship and your marriage. Confess these to one another, granting and receiving each other's forgiveness.

CHAPTER TEN

Faith vs. Fact

We live by faith, not by sight.

2 Corinthians 5:7 NIV

love faith. Life without faith is boring and empty. It becomes calculated
and measured. I hate calculated and measured because it guts the passion
and joy of experiencing life in the corners. By "life in the corners" I mean
that exhilarating feeling of leaning in and out of curves when I'm riding on a
motorcycle. You may not have experienced that but, suffice it to say, that is
where a motorcycle brings life. It's in the corners. It's leaning in and out and
becoming one with the power and engineering of the bike. It's like being on a
roller coaster!

Life can be like a motorcycle ride in a lot of ways. Not knowing what is
around the corner. Not knowing what it's going to feel like. None of us can pre-
dict what we are going to face around the next corner. But faith allows us to relax
and enjoy the ride rather than spoil the ride out of fear of the possibilities.

One alternative to living in faith is that people etch themselves into a controlled and measured life, trying to keep life on a straight highway and avoiding corners altogether. Ultimately this approach fails because we can't control what life is going to bring. (Plus it's no fun.)

Another approach that avoids faith is fear—always worrying about what is around the next corner. What kind of existence is that? This approach ultimately fails as well because we soon discover that all the worrying didn't stop life from happening or help in navigating the corners.

Faith is where it's at: Faith before the corners. Faith in the corners. Faith after the corners. Not faith in the facts, but faith in spite of the facts . . .

■ Facts and Truth

There is an important difference between facts and truth. Many of us have been educated to believe that facts are the truth because facts are the things we can prove empirically. Facts are the things we see with our eyes.

Truth, on the other hand, is what God sees and what God says. The *fact* of the matter is, I may face fear at times. The *truth* is I was made fearless.

For example, the fact that I got a "D" in my chemistry class in secondary school might have suggested to some at the time that I was lazy or unintelligent. But the truth was neither. If someone had bothered to look for the truth of what was going on in my life, they would have seen that my family was falling apart and that I was carrying enormous stress internally because of it.

How do we look past the facts (which are very real) and see the truth? We do it through faith. Faith is the lens through which we see the truth. Facts may be helpful at times but truth is power and life. Seeing is not believing. Believing is seeing.

Faith means "living as if it is true" (because it is)!

Taking a firm grip on hope, as we saw in the last chapter, is really important. But by itself, hope is not enough to build a high octane marriage in alignment with God's design. We cannot just *hope* that things will change. We must stand on that hope with acts of *faith*. Along with our hope, we must crank up the throttle on faith—action steps that trust the original design of our spouse. The Apostle Paul says it so clearly:

2 Corinthians 5:7

That is why we live by believing and not by seeing.

When a married couple starts life together, each spouse tends to see the other through the eyes of love, hope, and faith. However, it doesn't generally take long for the rose-colored glasses to come off and we find out who we really married—a real, live human being with failings, weaknesses, sins, and strongholds. But does faith *really* need to come crashing down when reality sets in? I don't believe so. As I stated earlier, faith is not rooted in the facts or in what we see. Faith is rooted in the truth, or what God sees.

This is a huge paradigm shift for most people. It means we have to look at each other through spiritual eyes and not natural eyes—not focusing on what we see with our earthly perspective, or on our own fears or history. Jesus showed us an example of how to do this when He prayed for His disciples:

John 17:6-9 NIV

I have revealed you to those whom you gave me out of the world. They were yours; you gave them to me and they have obeyed your word. Now

they know that everything you have given me comes from you. For I gave
them the words you gave me and they accepted them. They knew with
certainty that I came from you, and they believed that you sent me. I
pray for them. I am not praying for the world, but for those you have
given me, for they are yours (emphasis added).

I think it's pretty interesting in this passage that Jesus prayed in this way for His disciples just before most of them would abandon Him and flee, and Peter would flat-out deny even knowing Him.

"They have obeyed Your word."

"They know that everything you have given me comes from you."

"They knew with certainty that I came from you . . ."

The reality was, the disciples weren't exactly stellar followers. They jockeyed for position (Mk. 10:35-45), fell asleep on the job (Mk. 14:32-40), and often came up short in the faith department (Mt. 8:26, 16:8, 17:14-20). Those were the facts! But Jesus didn't go by the facts; He went by faith: Faith in what God had told Him about these men. Faith in God's design for them. And faith in God to work out that original design in them—regardless of what could be seen with the natural eyes.

■ Seeing through Eyes of Faith

We can learn to look at each other the way Jesus looked at His friends, and the way He now looks at His own bride, the Church. Really, the Church is in rough shape in many ways, isn't she? But Jesus doesn't see her that way. Scripture says, *"Christ loved the church and gave himself up for her to make her holy, cleansing her by the washing with water through the word, and to present her to himself as a radiant bride, without stain or wrinkle or any other blemish, but holy and blameless"* (Eph. 5:25-27). He doesn't focus on the mess she's in. He sees her holy, cleansed, radiant, unstained, unwrinkled, and blameless. (And by the way, He sees you and me that way, too!)

The Scripture goes on to say, *"In this same way, husbands ought to love their wives . . ."* (vs. 28). Now that's a powerful commandment! Part of it is no doubt the sacrificial commitment of a man's gatekeeping role. But another aspect is certainly the faith component which the husband can model, showing his wife and the rest of the family how to look not just at the facts, but at the truth—not just at "reality," but at God's original design.

How might it look in real life, for spouses to look at each other through eyes of faith? Let's look at a couple of possible scenarios:

Scenario #1

In a marriage where a husband is not leading the family, chances are the wife is. It is not enough merely to hope that he will start to lead. Faith takes the next step and says, "I believe that my hope is sure and I will depend upon Jesus to bring it to fruition. I will trust You, Lord, with my husband. My job is first to trust You, and second to trust him."

Taking the corners in faith for a <u>wife</u> in this scenario looks like:

1. Total faith in the Lord's leadership
2. Actually trusting the husband with a pure heart
3. Cheering him on even (and especially) when he fails, slips, or struggles
4. Operating in her own original design of joyful submission
5. Trusting that her obedience to the truth will promote transactional changes
6. Encouraging her husband
7. Interceding in prayer for her husband
8. Setting him up for success

The opposite of this would be a wife who operates in fear that leads to control which leads to frustration, exasperation, and withholding. The wife says to herself, "My future is not secure, therefore I will worry about it, stress about it, take over control, ride my husband about it, and complain to the Lord about it."

Taking the corners in faith by a <u>husband</u> in this situation looks like:

1. Total faith in the Lord's leadership
2. Speaking the truth in love about who she is (i.e. fearless, faith-filled, patient, etc.)
3. Leading in faith, truth, and action
4. Being willing to let things get worse before they get better by tolerating nothing less than her original design

The opposite of this would be a husband who operates in fear that leads to passivity which leads to the feeling of failure and the downward cycle of shame. The husband says to himself, "I will never get this right. I can't do it. I'm sick of failing. I would be better off not trying since it only leads to failure, and makes things worse when I don't follow through."

Scenario #2

In a marriage where the husband is operating in control and authoritarianism, chances are the wife is shut down and resigned with a cocktail of resentment, bitterness, and disappointment. Her heart becomes decayed and eventually impaired. We find that it can be difficult to reawaken a wife who has been beaten down with control and dominance. But with God all things are possible.

Taking the corners in faith for a wife in this situation looks like:

1. Absolute eyes fixed on God and establishing a heart connection with Him
2. Absolute faith in God that He can turn things around
3. Absolute belief in her original design and ability to live in her original design regardless of her husband's choices

The opposite of this would be the wife continuing to say to herself, "He will never change. It's not worth my effort to trust him, just to be crushed again. If I put my heart out there again I may never recover." It may include a wife telling her family and friends about how she is a victim of her husband's choices or allowing family and friends to curse or speak negatively about her husband.

Taking the corners in faith for a husband in this situation looks like:

1. Conviction and repentance over crushing his wife's spirit
2. Trusting the Lord for a revelation of what godly leadership actually looks like
3. Immediate attention given to recovering his wife's heart

The opposite of this would be a husband who operates in self-protection and is unwilling to let go of the need to dominate his wife. He may say to himself, "I only know one way to lead and it works for me. If I am not in control I don't know what to do. I don't know how to engage at the heart level and I don't have time for it. Can't we just make the most of it?"

Note that faith is not only aimed at how we see our spouse, but also at how we see ourselves. Faith is moving freely and forcefully into our own original design. God has spoken over each of our lives and declared who we are as His children—we are royalty; we are chosen; we are loved; we are fearless; we are powerful; we are called; we are capable—we should act like it!

■ Faith Rejects Fear

Most people don't realize how deeply fear is rooted in their daily lives. That's because the nature of fear is to *deceive* (mislead by a false appearance or statement; outwit, misrepresent, dupe, misinform, misdirect). Very often our fears sound logical to us. We think we're being prudent, cautious, or even righteous when what we are really operating in is flat-out fear!

You might be saying to yourself at this point, "Why is he focusing so much on fear? Can't we talk about something else?" The answer is, "No." And there is good reason. Fear is so prevalent in our lives that we are dulled to its presence. We are easily deceived by stress, worry, self-reliance, anxiety, anger and frustration—all of which are often symptoms of fear.

The Scriptures emphasize over and over again that the Lord wants us to be free of fear. As you step out of fear and into faith over your marriage, you can imagine God saying the same thing to you as He said to Joshua, *"Be strong and courageous. Do not be terrified; do not be discouraged, for the LORD your God will be with you wherever you go"* (Josh. 1:9 NIV).

You will gain increasing freedom from fear as you:

- allow the power of the Holy Spirit to uncover the presence of fear in your life,
- bring your fears to the cross through forgiveness and affirmation of the truth
- commit to take action to move in the opposite spirit.[16]

Does fear hold you back from operating in full faith over the facts of your marriage? Consider the following list and check any that may apply:

- ❏ Fear of failure (*"I know I am all those things but what if I can't live up to them?"*)

❏ Fear of success ("*I'm afraid of the next step/level,*" or "*How will everyone around me react to me?*" or "*What if I can't sustain the success?*")

❏ False humility (pride — "*Aw, shucks; I'm not all that.*")

❏ Unbelief ("*I don't believe I am powerful and fearless.*")

❏ Insecurity ("*I will only operate in the things people affirm and encourage me in.*")

❏ Rebellion ("*I don't think I can change,*" or "*That's just who I am,*" or "*That's just my personality,*" or "*I can't help it.*")

❏ Control ("*If I don't lead no one will,*" or "*If I don't take control here there will be chaos.*")

■ Faith Rejects Unbelief

It's all too easy to believe the lie that reality is defined by what we see, and that what we see with our eyes is the only reality. That's why we generally try all of the "fix it" counseling theories to improve communication in our marriage. The reality is that usually the root causes of our marriage issues are spiritually grounded and we cannot see them with our eyes. But because we don't want to deal with repentance and forgiveness, and the exposure of past hurts and pain and patterns, we often hide behind intellectualism and humanistic philosophies and strategies.

Unbelief shuts down the work of God in our lives.

This may sound like an odd assertion for me to make as a trained marriage and family counselor. But having counseled couples from both perspectives, I don't make the observation lightly. From my experience, I've seen that unbelief in the spiritual realm—and in God's healing power and authority—is a significant strategy of the devil. It shuts down a marriage by having us ignore the reality of the interplay between the physical realm and the spiritual realm in our lives and marriage. It leaves us powerless to change because communications counseling and other human philosophies cannot heal the deeper wounds that need God's power to heal through forgiveness and spiritual authority.

Unbelief fears . . .	Faith believes . . .
God doesn't	God does!
God can't	God can!
God won't	God will!

This is what unbelief does to a marriage:[17]

- Obstructs God's presence and power in our lives, and our ability to see God's presence and power in the life of our spouse
- Opens the door to taking offense, especially toward God, and many times toward those who are living in obedience to God. If our spouse is living in obedience and we are not, we take offense to his or her belief.
- Nurtures a root of skepticism
- Hinders prayer together and for each other
- Leads to instability and "cracks" in the foundation of the marriage
- Feeds a critical attitude toward one another
- Fosters arrogance and pride
- Causes each partner to hold up his/her standard as the superior one
- Brings discouragement to one another

Does unbelief hold you back from operating in full faith over the facts of your marriage? Consider the following list and check any that may apply:

❑ I find myself being disappointed—even offended—that God doesn't seem to work as I believe He should, or answer my prayers in the way I'd like—especially when it comes to my agenda for my spouse.

❑ When I hear of others' (or my spouse's) experiences of God's presence, power, or answered prayer, I am skeptical. My usual first reaction is to try to analyze or disprove their claim(s).

❑ I wonder why the Holy Spirit doesn't seem to talk to me or use me as powerfully as He uses my spouse.

❑ I tend to be self-sufficient and independent from my spouse; if I'm honest about it, I tend to be self-sufficient and independent from God.

❑ I first perceive people, including my spouse, and situations as "impossible" rather than "possible with God."

❑ I am not confident that I have spiritual authority through Jesus Christ.

❑ I am not motivated to pray consistently for my spouse, and I have little interest in intercessory or spiritual warfare prayer.

❑ Prayer is usually a last resort for me. I try to figure things out or work them out for myself first, My actions would indicate I believe that God helps those who help themselves (and sometimes I think my spouse needs to start helping himself/herself).

❑ I succumb to habitual behaviors and addictions (coping mechanisms) to comfort me when I feel discouraged, afraid, hopeless, hurt, etc. and am not willing to believe/see the effect on my spouse.

❑ I think my situation, my sins, my fears, my marriage, my spiritual life, my _____ (fill in the blank) will never change.

❑ I tend to be worried, fearful, and anxious about the spiritual development of my spouse—like it just won't happen.

❑ I try to control my spouse, situations, and even God, because I am afraid to let go and trust God to do it.

■ Exercising Faith through Practical Action

Acts of faith are practical steps toward operating in one's original design and relating to others in the same way, regardless of any results. That means you may step out in faith instead of the facts, operate according to the truth and not by what you see with your natural eyes, and then not see any changes at first. In that place, you do not lose hope. You do not lose faith. You exercise your faith just the way you would any other muscle, by using it over and over again. You don't allow the disappointment of failure and defeat keep you or your spouse from holding fast to faith and staying on the path to breakthrough.

Affirmation is one practical faith-action step that is easy to implement. Whenever, and as often as is possible, verbally affirm your spouse with God's love, care, design, and purpose for him (or her). Find ways to notice aspects of his or her original design, and point them out. Your words are powerful. They have the capacity for bringing life or death (Prov. 18:21). When you use them to impart life, you bring a blessing to your husband or wife through the power of your words.

Through the spoken word, you can bring God's reality into your reality. He is the God who gives life to the dead and calls things that are not as though they were (Rom. 4:17). You can imitate this faith component of God's character when you declare the truths of what He says about your husband or wife. Affirmation is one of the ways you can help your spouse become who God destined him or her to be. In fact, doing so is part of *your* original design!

1 Thessalonians 5:11 NIV

Therefore encourage one another and build each other up, just as in fact you are doing.

Affirmation ("words of life") might look like:

"Darling, I love the way God made you. Your original design is amazing. Your strength and leadership is the glue that holds this family together. I don't know what I'd do without you. I love how you love Jesus and are committed to following Him, and that you are taking me with you as you do. I see His wisdom and compassion in you. I learn from you every day. I'm so glad you're YOU!"

Try to think of creative ways to affirm your husband or wife. Something like the above paragraph could be spoken face-to-face, or written in a card and tucked into a lunch, a pocket, or a purse/briefcase to be discovered by surprise later in the day . You can text an affirming statement by cell phone or send an email. You can speak it first thing in the morning or last thing before you go to bed at night. It can be one sentence, five sentences, or even just three words: YOU ARE AMAZING!

■ Exercising Faith through Forgiveness

Another practical faith-action step is both granting and receiving forgiveness. As we have seen (and practiced) several times in this book, breakthrough in marriage comes through genuine repentance along with extending forgiveness. Being able to grant genuine forgiveness is a faith step because it means entrusting the offender to God and not extracting our own judgment or punishment. It means releasing him or her from the debt owed to us, without any guarantee that we will be (or feel) recompensed in this lifetime. Forgiveness sees not the facts of the offense, but the truth of who the person is behind the offense, and how God sees him or her through eyes of mercy.

For many of us, granting forgiveness is easier than receiving it. In our time, the enemy has raised up the lie that chronic sorrow, guilt, regret, and shame are more honorable and appropriate than freedom from past mistakes. Others use the facts against us and we begin to believe that the facts of our past define us. Consequently, many are shackled and controlled by the spirit of shame.

Nothing could be further from the truth. God defines us by our original design. That is the truth! We need to appropriate the truth of the power of genuine repentance and learn to *receive* forgiveness as well as extend it, and believe the truth of our original design. The transactional effect of these principles will be evidenced by future actions, changes of heart and patterns, and sacrifice.

■ Exercising Faith through Prayer

Besides taking practical action steps, another powerful way to exercise the faith muscle and practice seeing your spouse through spiritual eyes is by prayer, specifically through intercession. To intercede means "to act or interpose in behalf of someone in difficulty or trouble, as by pleading or petition, to attempt to reconcile differences between two people or groups, to mediate."[18] Through prayer, you have an incredible opportunity and privilege (and platform, as a spouse) to partner with God in seeing His original design for your husband or wife come to fruition. There are multiple creative ways to do this, but essentially your intercession should include:

a. **Hearing God's voice in prayer**—ask God to show you His perspective. Ask Him specific questions and allow the Holy Spirit to speak to you through the Scriptures, impressions in your spirit, mental pictures, or through other people. He may even speak to you in a dream! The Holy Spirit speaks to us in many ways when we ask Him.[19]

b. **Intercessory prayer**—commit to praying regularly *for* the realization and accomplishment of God's design in your spouse's life.

c. **Spiritual warfare prayer**—use your authority in Christ *against* the schemes of the enemy that seek to oppose, corrupt, and pervert God's original design. Contend for that design. The enemy hates the truth. Declare it aloud in Jesus' name, rebuking all activity and assignments against your spouse. "Resist the devil," Scripture tells us, "and he will flee" (Jas. 4:7).

In Chapter Six, I introduced you to Paul and Jennifer. They were the couple who told us that "God turned their upside-down marriage right-side up." What I didn't tell you in that chapter was the huge role that prayer—particularly intercession and spiritual warfare prayer—played in their marriage restoration.

Jennifer, when she looked at Paul at the very beginning of their efforts to re-align their marriage to God's design, really couldn't see the things that God said about him. Because she had so many times felt let down and on her own, it was difficult for her to set aside her independence and trust Paul to initiate (and follow through) with his leadership responsibilities in the home. Paul, because he had so often felt his efforts were criticized and under-appreciated by Jennifer, really couldn't see the things God said about Jennifer, either. He was reluctant to put himself out there to lead, for fear she would not receive it and there would be conflict.

Jennifer began to keep a journal. In it, she wrote down components of Paul's original design, and Scripture verses that spoke to God's design for Paul's life and role as a husband. She recorded her conversations with God as she interceded for her husband to begin to walk in the things God said about him. When she felt tempted to take matters into her own hands in various situations, she ran to her journal, pulled it out, and re-affirmed in her heart and mind what the TRUTH was. Those truths helped her be patient and not try to "fix" situations or take back the reins of control. They helped her talk to God about her concerns in prayer, and not to have to mention every little thing to Paul.

Paul was also having trouble believing the things God said about his wife's original design. He doubted she could ever learn to trust him and let him take care of things in his own way and at his own pace. But he, too, also learned to make prayer an important part of his efforts to improve his marriage. When he could see fear and an independent spirit moving in to steal his wife's peace, he learned to see past the circumstances and recognize who and what the true enemy was—and take authority over it through prayer.

Remarkably, things started to turn around in their marriage as each of them learned to talk to God in prayer about their concerns, not necessarily always to each other. As spiritual transactions took place in the heavenly realms through intercession and spiritual warfare, change and growth occurred in the natural realm. That's the power of prayer in faith!

I John 5:14-15 NIV

This is the confidence we have in approaching God: that if we ask anything according to his will, he hears us. And if we know that he hears us—whatever we ask—we know that we have what we asked of him.

TIME TO DRIVE—Practical Application Exercise for Couples

Now it's your turn. Take some time for reflection. Identify the facts about your marriage that characterize the way you have been operating outside of God's design. Another way to think about it is, "If I could change something about my marriage what would it be?" Or, "What areas of my marriage are less than great and what would it look like if they *were* great?" Or, "What areas of our marriage can we (or do we) NOT talk about?"

Then, for each area of your marriage that comes to mind, ask yourself, "What is the truth?" For example, if the fact is that you cannot agree on how to parent your kids, ask the question, "What is the truth about our marriage regarding agreement on parenting?" The truth is you were designed for agreement and unity. You were designed as a team with different gifts to complement each other and your kids will be the beneficiaries. The truth is that what you agree on together will be better than any approach determined by either of you in isolation.

You are not designed to operate apart. The real issue is not a disagreement about parenting but a refusal to accept, agree, and operate in God's design for your marriage, which is to sit down and spend as much time as it takes to agree on parenting objectives and a plan. The facts may be, "We will never agree." Faith says, "God designed us to agree so let's trust Him and go for it!"

1. Together with your spouse, repent before God and each other of any areas of believing the facts about your marriage as if they were truth. Get forgiveness done and get the healing started. God can do it.

2. Declare the truth about each circumstance where the facts have carried the day and kept your marriage from unity and life.

3. Take each area identified and write a new chapter built upon faith in God's design—faith in the truth of who He created you and your marriage to be. Consider keeping a prayer journal or log in which to record your prayers and affirmations of faith as you are both growing into your original design, and into alignment with God's will for your life and marriage.

CHAPTER ELEVEN

Breaking the Power of the Secret

But if we walk in the light, as he is in the light,
we have fellowship with one another,
and the blood of Jesus, his Son, purifies us from all sin.

I JOHN 1:7

Barely able to share with a prayer team of men because he was so racked with shame, my friend reluctantly told us his secret—a secret that was destroying him from the inside out. After he shared his secret, I told him he needed to come clean with his wife.

"I could never do that," he said. "I don't know if my wife could deal with it. I am afraid what will happen."

I told him his marriage was running on lies and deception and he would never find breakthrough until he came into the light and trusted the Lord in the consequences. To his credit, he told his wife the truth. She forgave him and today they are living in the light with a marriage in alignment with God's design. They are experiencing the power of a high octane marriage.

I have yet to see a spouse who would not forgive another spouse who broke the power of the secret with humility and genuine repentance—and I have seen the worst of secrets revealed. I believe this is because God honors the light; that is where He works. He gives grace to the offended and strength to the offender to overcome the loss of trust that comes from holding secrets.

Because biblical marriage is such a powerful tool in God's Kingdom, it is greatly opposed by the enemy. Marriage in God's design is extremely powerful. A marriage operating in unity is a formidable force for the Kingdom because God's glory and economy for relationship is witnessed between husband and wife. Because of this, there are some specific demonic schemes that mean to divide marriages and families and tear down God's Kingdom work. One such scheme I call the power of the secret.

■ The Power of the Secret

"If I tell my husband the truth, he'll leave me."

"What she doesn't know won't hurt her."

"Why do I need to dig all that up again?"

Secrets play right into Satan's schemes. A secret is the truth concealed—hidden in darkness. It is precisely in the darkness where Satan does his best work. Because he is the prince of darkness, he functions well in that environment. However, we cannot see in the darkness. Our vision is blocked and we are completely vulnerable to deception.

Whenever we agree with Satan by operating
in darkness we give access to his voice of deception
and a spirit of oppression.

The key lies that Satan uses to imprison us when we come into agreement with the power of the secret are:

- fear of exposure
- condemnation
- fear of losing our reputation
- fear of judgment
- failure
- shame
- insecurity
- pride
- control

The power of the secret is a double-bind. We don't want to carry the fear, shame, and guilt of our sin, but we are afraid of disclosure because we are ashamed. And so, we live with secrets that become poison and slowly eat away at our hearts and our marriage.

I remember the feeling of complete failure and fear that made me feel I needed to take my secrets to the grave. I was willing to carry the burden of the secret in order to spare Amy the pain of broken trust and disappointment or risk the loss of my marriage. But the weight of the secret became unbearable. I believe that weight was God's grace in my life at that time telling me to break the lie and deceit. One day I did—and that started the greatest adventure of our marriage, an adventure that Amy and I would not trade for anything. What the Lord has taught us really saved our marriage. Make no mistake, it was hard at times. But it was also worth it—a hundred times over.

■ Living in the Light

The only way to break the deadly pattern of secrecy is to "live in the light" and come clean with our spouse. In virtually all the cases I am aware of, the honest disclosure of secrets has brought healing and trust and reconciliation to marriages.

What we are most interested in are the truth and transactions that prohibit secrets from forming, and crushes them if they have already formed. We find this core truth in Scripture:

1 John 1:5-10

This is the message he has given us to announce to you: God is light and there is no darkness in him at all. So we are lying if we say we have fellowship with God but go on living in spiritual darkness. We are not living in the truth. But if we are living in the light of God's presence, just as Christ is, then we have fellowship with each other, and the blood of Jesus, his Son, cleanses us from every sin. If we say we have no sin, we are only fooling ourselves and refusing to accept the truth. But if we confess our sins to him, he is faithful and just to forgive us and to cleanse us from every wrong. If we claim we have not sinned, we are calling God a liar and showing that his word has no place in our hearts.

No relationship can survive, much less thrive, without trust.

**Perfection is not required for a
high octane marriage—honesty is.**

The agreement to live 100% in the light is critical to experiencing the power of God's design for marriage. Living one hundred percent in the light means there are no secrets. There are no past secrets and no present secrets and there is a constant stream of staying current and guarding the trust of living in the light.

Jesus made it very clear that light and darkness cannot live together. He taught that darkness leads to deception, death, and destruction. He exhorted His followers that God's children should have nothing to do with operating in the darkness:

John 8:12

Jesus said to the people, "I am the light of the world. If you follow me, you won't be stumbling through the darkness, because you will have the light that leads to life."

Ephesians 5:3-4, 8-13

Let there be no sexual immorality, impurity, or greed among you. Such sins have no place among God's people. Obscene stories, foolish talk, and coarse jokes—these are not for you . . . For though your hearts were once full of darkness, now you are full of light from the Lord, and your behavior should show it! For this light within you produces only what is good and right and true. Try to find out what is pleasing to the Lord. Take no part in the worthless deeds of evil and darkness; instead, rebuke and expose them. It is shameful even to talk about the things that ungodly people do in secret. But when the light shines on them, it becomes clear how evil these things are. And where your light shines, it will expose their evil deeds.

John 8:43-44

Why can't you understand what I am saying? It is because you are unable to do so! For you are the children of your father the Devil, and you love to do the evil things he does. He was a murderer from the beginning and has always hated the truth. There is no truth in him. When he lies, it is consistent with his character; for he is a liar and the father of lies.

■ Breaking the Power of the Secret

When we recognize that operating in agreement with Jesus and His word will ultimately bring healing and life (Jn. 8:12; 1 Jn. 1:7), and operating in agreement with Satan will bring about destruction and a slow and painful death, we can muster the strength to say, "Enough is enough. The temporary excruciating pain of revealing the truth is better than the oppressive pain of living a lie as a hypocrite." A decision for obedience to Christ or obedience to Satan is at hand.

For a marriage to be in alignment, there are no options.

Some couples have attempted selective disclosure. That is, they have determined which secrets should be shared and which should not. This approach leaves a marriage artificially secure. The foundation contains cracks of deception that will crumble under the pressures of life and marriage. This approach, while more comfortable, is really providing false comfort. When the unshared secret finally surfaces down the road, the pain will be deeper because of the missed opportunity to disclose sooner. Even if the secret never surfaces, the poison of hypocrisy will compromise any real establishment of trust and the marriage will never be in alignment. In my experience, it is impossible to keep deception hidden. It will always find a way to bring destruction to a marriage.

The process of exposing secrets is important. One helpful principle is to be thorough and general. For example, if your worst secret is that you are hooked on ice cream and every day you sneak a pint of Ben & Jerry's Chunky Monkey®, then the important parts of the disclosure are:

- "hooked" (not excusing or downplaying the sin—calling it what it is)
- "every day" (not excusing or justifying or understating the frequency)
- "sneak" (not ignoring the deceptive component)

On these elements we want to be thorough. Whether you eat Chunky Monkey® or New York Super Fudge Chunk ® may not be important. Sometimes we can "feed" on spending too much time and energy on the specifics of past sin and secrets, and actually give the enemy access to the discussion. What is critical is that the behavior (the sin) is exposed. As you begin the process of coming clean, the Lord will likely heighten your sensitivity to elements of the secret that need to be shared, elements to which you were previously oblivious.

It is also important that the behavior (sin and secret) be hated. Repentance is what is needed, not mere confession. The difference is that repentance includes confession *and* obedience—the commitment and desire to change permanently at all personal cost. The absence of a heart of repentance in the disclosure of secrets will undermine the healing because it is hypocrisy. Hypocrisy is deception. Such efforts are religious and not transactional in the spiritual realm.

■ Breaking the Power of Shame

Shame is a powerful bondage of the enemy that keeps people locked down under the power of the secret. Shame is a scheme of the enemy to steal the transformational power of God's forgiveness (and the forgiveness of others) and to nullify the power of the cross.

The following is excerpted from Stormie Omartian's book, *Lord, I Want to Be Whole*. I include it here because it is such an accurate description of what it feels like to be caught in—and to walk out of—the enemy's stronghold of shame:

> "It's especially important to include every sexual sin you have ever committed," my counselor Mary Anne had instructed me the first time I saw her, when she asked me to go home and list my sins.

How embarrassing, I thought. My desperate need for love, approval, and closeness had been so strong that I'd fallen into one wrong relationship after another. It would be mortifying to tell her about all that.

"You don't have to go into any detail," Mary Anne added, as if she knew exactly what I was thinking. "Just put down the name, confess your involvement, and ask God to restore you. We'll pray over the whole list next time."

As I left her office I immediately started remembering various instances, and each one made me cringe. I found it felt good to write it on my "sin list," confessing it to God and asking forgiveness just as she told me to do, like the release that comes from telling a bad secret. I had confessed it. God had forgiven it. I felt cleansed and new.[20]

Obviously, not all shameful secrets are sexual in nature. And no sin—sexual or otherwise—is worse than another. Sexual sin is not more heinous to God than lying, cheating, or stealing. Immorality is not more reprehensible than gossip or anger. However, generally speaking, some sins do have more dramatic and personal consequences than others.

Scripture says, *"Flee from sexual immorality. All other sins a man commits are outside his body, but he who sins sexually sins against his own body"* (1 Cor. 6:18 NIV). If I steal money, I can give it back. If I gossip about someone, I can go tell him or her I'm sorry, and have it be forgiven and forgotten. But there's just something about sexual sin that sticks to us. For many, it becomes like a stain that can never be rubbed off. That stain is *shame.*

Do you have a secret—ANY secret? It could be issues with addictions, financial mismanagement, or untruths that you have told. Do you struggle with a pervading sense of shame and worthlessness as a result? Consider the following list; see if any apply. If they do, take some time with the Lord to bring your secret out into the light with Him, and receive His full forgiveness.

- ❏ I feel like I am constantly living with a secret that I am afraid others will find out about.
- ❏ I am unable to form close, trusting friendships and relationships.
- ❏ I live in fear of rejection if this secret is discovered.
- ❏ I do not believe God can ever fully forgive my sin.
- ❏ I do not believe my friends, husband, parents, church family, etc. can ever understand or forgive my sin.
- ❏ I struggle with inferiority.
- ❏ I have low self-worth/self-image.
- ❏ I suffer condemnation, and from what seem to be voices in my head telling me that I am worthless and will never deserve love, that I will never amount to anything.
- ❏ I cannot forgive myself.
- ❏ I constantly battle tormenting thoughts and memories about my sin, or about the relationships and circumstances surrounding it.
- ❏ I have nightmares.
- ❏ I believe I am "damaged goods;" I can never be completely whole or pure again.
- ❏ I do not believe I can ever have a healthy, satisfying marriage.

■ What Does Shame Look Like in Marriage?

Consider the ways that shame may be playing out in your relationship with your husband or wife. Again, prayerfully go through the list and check any that apply. Then go back to the Lord in prayer, receiving His forgiveness and seeking His direction for how you should go about bringing your shame and your secret into the light with your spouse.

DEFEAT

Believing lies of the past:
- ❏ "I am no good. The past sins of my own and my family of origin define me. I will always struggle with this sin. "

Believing lies of the present:
- ❏ Discouraged, fearful, hiding thoughts and feelings of remorse and regret

Believing lies of the future:
- ❏ "My marriage can never get any better. I've blown it too many times."

ISOLATION

- ❏ Believing the lie that I am in this life alone and no one will ever *really* know me and all my sin and still love me

WITHHOLDING

- ❏ Believing the lie that you are not deserving of being fully loved, so you withhold fully loving
- ❏ Believing the lie that you are not deserving of full joy after what you have done and therefore cannot bring full joy into the marriage. You don't even know what joy really is or how it feels
- ❏ Being unable to share your heart completely because guilt and shame occupy so much territory of the heart (secrets)

❏ Believing the lie that you are "damaged goods" and don't get to have dreams come true, so you withhold sharing dreams

❏ Believing the lie that after what you have done, you don't deserve affection/intimacy, so you self-protect by withholding in those areas

As long our sins and our shame remain in the dark, they are a part of Satan's kingdom. He has jurisdiction over them—a legal right, so to speak. But when we confess our sins and bring them out into the light, we break the hold Satan has over them. We are forgiven. We are cleansed. We are restored. *"If we confess our sins, he is faithful and just and will forgive us our sins and purify us from all unrighteousness." (1 Jn. 1:9)*

God wants His children to be released from the power of the secret and the bondage of shame. Living 100% in the light with God and each other is part of our original design. In Jesus Christ, all things are made new!

2 Corinthians 5:17 NIV

Therefore, if anyone is in Christ, he is a new creation; the old has gone, the new has come!

■ Experiencing God's Design: Living 100 % in the Light

What do we say to ourselves to justify keeping the secret?

⇒ "It's my sin, my business."

⇒ "It's my issue."

⇒ "What good is that going to do?"

⇒ "The past is the past."

⇒ "He/she may not love me the same."

⇒ "I don't want to disappoint him/her."

⇒ "I don't want my spouse to have a tarnished image of me."

⇒ "It will only hurt him/her."

These kind of self-talk statements are a smokescreen of the enemy to keep you from knowing the truth. Think of it this way instead: Consider the picture of a tiger approaching a person in a chair. That person is getting ready to come into the light with his or her spouse about a secret, and there is fear of being devoured. To the person's great surprise, the tiger just starts licking him and making him (or her) laugh! *What on earth was I afraid of?* the person asks . . .

There is actually joy and intimacy in being fully known!

This was a picture the Lord showed Amy and me as we were working with one husband through the fear of coming into the light with his wife. It really helped him work through the fear of disclosure. He was relieved to find out that on the other side of the disclosure, there truly was relief, forgiveness, and freedom from the power of the secret!

Although the person hearing the secret will not likely actually laugh and enjoy the disclosure (which is not the point), in our experience, spouses have most often responded in grace and forgiveness when a secret is shared sensitively, remorsefully, and thoroughly without justification for the sin.

Following is an example of how to share and hear a secret based upon the ice cream example mentioned earlier:

Husband: Honey, can we get some time to talk? I have something I want to discuss with you.

Wife: Sure.

Husband: I have been hiding something from you for some time and I want to bring it into the light and seek your forgiveness. For the past two years, I have been sneaking a pint of ice cream every day behind your back. I have become hooked on this habit and have I been living a lie and breaking your trust. I know that this habit is unhealthy for me and I take full responsibility for my actions and my sin of deception, lying, and betraying your trust. It is my absolute commitment to break this habit immediately and do whatever it takes to rebuild your trust. I commit to living 100% in the light from here forward. I will need your support, accountability, and encouragement if you are willing. I am so sorry for not telling you sooner. I am so sorry I betrayed your trust. I want our marriage to always be 100% in the light. Will you please forgive me?

Wife: I forgive you. I forgive you completely and permanently. It's not okay to lie and we can't live with secrets. It is hard to know that you have been sneaking behind my back and lying to my face. It really hurts to know that this has been going on and I may need some time to heal from this. But thank you for bringing it into the light and thank you for your desire to change. I may need time for us to rebuild trust. I will need you to hold to your commitment and always live 100% in the light with me. As hard as this is, I choose to work with you to rebuild trust in our marriage based upon both of us living in the light.

Usually, there is a need to rebuild trust after a session like this. Many believe that rebuilding trust is a long and difficult and maybe even impossible process. That simply isn't true. There is a sure-fire way to rebuild trust:

Make a promise and keep it.

When we make a promise and keep it, it automatically builds trust. In fact, it can't help but build trust. When making a promise, it is important to promise things we can fulfill, and to put supportive elements in place to make sure we are capable of keeping our promise. In the ice cream example, the corresponding promise might be, "I promise not to eat any ice cream today." In this case, I have made a promise with a limited time frame that allows me to have a victory and begin to build trust with my first success. Obviously, keeping my promise for one day will not rebuild all of the trust that is lost, but it is an important start. In addition to making the promise, I will also clear out all ice cream from my freezer, as well as stay away from any store that sells ice cream. I may have to do this for some time. I will make the same promise each day and after awhile, I will make a weekly promise, then a monthly promise, and so forth.

It is also important to note that breaking a promise will usually compromise trust at a faster rate than keeping promises can rebuild it. So, success in keeping the promises that are made is essential. It is also important for the person receiving the promises to maintain a heart condition of grace and operate from an intentional posture of encouragement and confidence that the spouse will keep his or her promises.

TIME TO DRIVE—Practical Application Exercise for Couples

■ Breaking the Power of Secrets and Shame

Breaking the power of the secret can be an intimidating idea. We have placed this chapter near the end of the book so that before tackling it, you would have time to build up alignment and truth and begin to experience the Life in the Kingdom that comes with alignment.

There is no high octane marriage where there are secrets. You may think that you are successfully keeping your secret. You may think that it is stored so deep down inside that no one will ever know. But you're wrong. It is an inevitable reality that a secret can be demonically energized and therefore toxic, and the only medicine that can de-toxify the power of the secret is light. There is no other way out, so you might as well do it now.

I can't even begin to count the number of couples who have chosen to get everything in the light and later said it was the thing that either saved or changed their marriage forever. So if you really want a high octane marriage, punch the gas on this one and make it count!

1. Sit together and share any secrets that stand between you. Ask for and grant forgiveness with each other for each secret revealed. Leave no stone unturned; otherwise this exercise will be for nothing.

2. Pray together and apply the transformational truths (4 R's) to each of the secrets revealed. Don't just name the behavior. Ask the Lord to show you the strongholds fueling that behavior (e.g. pride, independence, self-indulgence, lust, deception, materialism, insecurity . . . or whatever they may be). Name each stronghold issue separately as you work through the 4R prayer model.

3. Identify any and all areas of shame, self-condemnation, self-hatred, and regret. Apply the 4R's to each one. Treat shame, self-condemnation, self-hatred, and regret as sin. Each of these sins disagrees with God about who He created you to be.

4. Make a declaration of faith that you each agree with God about your original design(s), with His design for your marriage, and that you are bringing your marriage into alignment with that design. Affirm that

each of you is a child of God, adopted into His family, royalty, forgiven, redeemed and restored, a new creation. He will bring healing and take care of your past. He designed you for purpose and mission and is restoring you to that purpose.

5. Saturate your mind with Scripture. Post truths and Bible verses where you are likely to see and read them often. Know the truth of those Scriptures and know the truth of the many saints who failed and yet Jesus forgave them, restored them, and used them to advance His kingdom and purposes.

6. Stay in the light daily. Communicate with each other about all ways the enemy tried to defeat you with lies that day. Pray through any "open doors" and close them through transactional prayer.

7. Agree on a weekly plan to check in with each other and pray through any issues that may surface after breaking the power of the secret and following your agreement to live in the light.

CHAPTER TWELVE

Becoming Unoffendable

You must make allowance for each other's faults
and forgive the person who offends you.
Remember, the Lord forgave you, so you must forgive others.

COLOSSIANS 3:13

There is nothing scarier than hitting a slippery spot on the road on your motorcycle at high speed. A painted line or a spot of grease can change your life in split second. That is not the kind of excitement and exhilaration we are going for. We want a life-giving high octane adventure in our marriage, not a fear-induced injection of adrenaline!

Amy and I have learned a lot on our road to a high octane marriage, the high points of which we have shared with you in this book. One more key component we have found over the years, though, is that of learning to become "unoffendable." That's not actually a real word but we have adopted it because of the power of its truth. Taking offense to injustices in a marriage is the equivalent of a high speed hazard on the road. It will take the wheels right out from under you and spoil your adventure in the blink of an eye.

Taking offense when we are mistreated is a road hazard worth avoiding at all cost. "Wait a second!" you might say. "Why can't I take offense when I am mistreated? Am I not justified in my anger when I experience injustice? Am I not entitled to retaliate when my spouse is dishing out poisonous words at me?"

Here's the answer: *Perhaps by the world's standards, but not in God's Kingdom.*

Jesus modeled for us what it looks like to become unoffendable. He didn't react when he was treated unjustly. He didn't defend himself when he was falsely accused. He didn't strike back when he was stricken time and time again. He didn't lash out when he was being lashed with shards of glass and metal. The accounts we find in Scripture tell it all:

1 Peter 2:23

He did not retaliate when he was insulted, nor threaten revenge when he suffered. He left his case in the hands of God, who always judges fairly.

Philippians 2:6-8

Though he was God, he did not demand and cling to his rights as God. He made himself nothing; he took the humble position of a slave and appeared in human form. And in human form he obediently humbled himself even further by dying a criminal's death on a cross.

It's important to note that the verses preceding both of these passages tell us to follow Jesus with the same attitude he had (emphasis added):

1 Peter 2:20-21

But if you suffer for doing good and endure it patiently, God is pleased with you. For God called you to do good, even if it means suffering, just as Christ suffered for you. He is your example, and you must follow in his steps.

Philippians 2:5

Your attitude should be the same that Christ Jesus had.

If Jesus Himself did not cling to His rights, how can we?

The Bible exhorts us to waive all of our rights, relinquish them completely, and become nothing. This is one of the most difficult things to do—especially in the face of injustice. I recognize that this is completely counterintuitive in our culture and in our day. But it is also the truth. I am not making this stuff up. God has laid it out for us in living color.

Everything in us wants to defend, justify, retaliate, and exact revenge on all who would dare offend us, doesn't it? Most of us wear invisible buttons on our sleeve that merely need to be pushed and a predictable reaction will immediately ensue. Most of us know the buttons operating in those closest to us, especially our spouses. We leverage them to get our way or to get a reaction that will expose the vulnerabilities of our spouse. How caveman is that?

But what if you didn't have any buttons? What if there were no buttons for anyone to push? What if, in response to unfair circumstances, unkind words, unjust accusations, and provocative animosity you just "took it?" What if you first checked your heart to see if there was any real truth to what was being said or done to you? What if there *was* some truth and you simply took responsibility for it and humbly asked for forgiveness?

On the other hand, what if there wasn't any truth to it and you immediately forgave that person for the injustice? What if you chose to let God defend, justify, retaliate, and exact revenge if He saw fit to do so?

Romans 12:17-21

Never pay back evil for evil to anyone. Do things in such a way that everyone can see you are honorable. Do your part to live in peace with everyone, as much as possible. Dear friends, never avenge yourselves. Leave that to God. For it is written, "I will take vengeance; I will repay those who deserve it," says the Lord. Instead, do what the Scriptures say: "If your enemies are hungry, feed them. If they are thirsty, give them something to drink, and they will be ashamed of what they have done to you." Don't let evil get the best of you, but conquer evil by doing good.

Luke 6:27-33

But if you are willing to listen, I say, love your enemies. Do good to those who hate you. Pray for the happiness of those who curse you. Pray for those who hurt you. If someone slaps you on one cheek, turn the other cheek. If someone demands your coat, offer your shirt also. Give what you have to anyone who asks you for it; and when things are taken away from you, don't try to get them back. Do for others as you would like them to do for you. Do you think you deserve credit merely for loving those who love you? Even the sinners do that! And if you do good only to those who do good to you, is that so wonderful? Even sinners do that much!

This is what it sounds like and looks like to become unoffendable!

There is no freedom like the freedom that comes from being able to resist a reaction. Indeed, the ability to consider a choice in response to our circumstances is one of the most important distinctions between us and animals. Yet, how often do we let our circumstances or injustices dictate our joy, happiness, mood, or life? The truth is that we have the ability to choose. God has given us the capacity to choose our response to life and its hurts, wounds, and injustices. We are not relegated to a justifiable knee-jerk reaction to protect ourselves and strike back at an offender. In fact, our responses to injustices may be the best indicators of our true heart condition.

■ Expectations

To add insult to injury, in our experience, the marriage relationship is the place where most people experience the strongest feelings and reactions to injustice. This is probably due to our expectations in marriage. We expect to be treated better within our marriage. We expect to be free from false accusations and unkind words in our marriage so, when they hit, they hit harder. This means that becoming unoffendable to our spouse may be the best measure of our trust in God.

When we choose humility, grace, and forgiveness over retaliation, bitterness and resentment, we demonstrate a deep capacity for trusting God to defend, protect, and sustain us. Becoming unoffendable has everything to do with trusting God. Becoming unoffendable has everything to do with humility and letting God have complete control of my life.

I think God lives within faith and humility. Wherever He finds faith, there He lives. Wherever He finds humility, there He stays. The converse is true as well. Wherever God smells unbelief, He is gone. Wherever God sees pride, He disappears and lets us enjoy boosting ourselves.

If we want to cultivate and sustain a high octane marriage, it's imperative that we cultivate and sustain the capacity of becoming unoffendable. Remember at the beginning of this book where I said that there were original design components that would be true of all of us, while some would be true just for individuals? This is one of those components that God intends to be true for ALL of us. God's original design is for each one of us to be conformed to the image of His Son Jesus—and Jesus was unoffendable. Therefore, becoming unoffendable is a part of God's design for each and every one of His children.

This singular truth has the power to transform a marriage. Perhaps it is because when we become unoffendable, we become like Jesus. And there's no power like Jesus' power!

■ What Does It *Look* Like?

Becoming unoffendable requires us to:

1. Relinquish our rights
2. Abandon our entitlements
3. Hold our expectations loosely
4. Eliminate our reactions to injustice
5. Let God defend us
6. Let God comfort us
7. Let God deal with the other person
8. Forgive immediately and without condition

Can I be dead honest with you here? Amy and I don't ever want to come across like we think we've arrived, or that we're perfect people. Far from it. We still mess up. We still let each other down from time to time. We still have misunderstandings and occasional hurts between us, despite all efforts to the opposite. That's just life.

But something is different now, since we've learned the powerful principle of being unoffendable. Those disappointments, misunderstandings, and even hurts don't have the power to take us off the road anymore. And because each of us has the confidence that the other will not take an offense when we mess up, our trust and intimacy factor has skyrocketed. It's an incredibly freeing feeling to have the confidence that your honey's not going to hold a grudge—ever. Not going to try and get back at you—ever. And not going to make you pay a cost for your mistakes—ever.

That's true freedom. True alignment. True power! And it's a hallmark of a high octane marriage.

■ About What I Didn't Say

While I was writing this book, numerous people asked me, "Are you going to have a chapter on communication? How about intimacy? Will you talk about parenting or finances?" To each of these suggestions, I said, "No."

I said "No" because of my core belief that those "topics" are never really the problem in a troubled marriage. We may *think* they are the problem. We go to counselors and pastors and tell them we have a problem "communicating" or "parenting," or that we have an "intimacy" problem. But I don't think those are the root causes of tension and disunity in marriages. They are just symptoms. The "presenting problem" is usually a "presenting *symptom*." The real problem is generally a "heart" issue.

In my experience, when we apply the biblical truths God has given us for an abundant life of freedom and unity, we will be addressing the real problems in our relationship—and the symptoms will take care of themselves. For example, when a husband and wife begin to take the time to learn and share the depths of their hearts for each other, communication issues will dissolve. Try it—you'll see. When husbands and wives take the time to genuinely repent and forgive each other of past hurts, mistakes and injustices, intimacy will no doubt begin to heat up. I've seen it time and time again.

Bottom line: If we address spiritual root issues in our hearts and relationships, appropriating God's gift of the power of the Cross and His Holy Spirit, we will find new life and new marriages.

When a "problem" presents itself, don't settle for simply trying to cure the symptom. Look deeper into the spiritual roots beneath the symptom to bring powerful and permanent healing. Now you know how.

■ A Final Word

The primary purpose for building a high octane marriage is not just to make your life better (although it no doubt will!). The principles Amy and I have shared with you do not constitute a self-help remedy. The purpose in building a high octane marriage is to fulfill God's design, bring Him glory, and advance His kingdom. That's a high calling and a high privilege, with exponential ramifications.

Marriages that reflect God's Kingdom life of power, joy, and unity have a supernatural impact on their kids, their families, their friends, their churches, and their communities. These "high octane" marriages have the power and authority to exercise the ministry of Jesus to the world. They are packed with credibility and spiritual authority. They are in alignment with the truth of Jesus Christ and are set free to set others free.

We were created, you and I, to live Kingdom life and bring Kingdom life to others. That's what a high octane marriage is all about. God's grace and power be upon you as you pursue your own calling to a high octane marriage. Zoom, zoom, zoom!

TIME TO DRIVE—Practical Application Exercise for Couples

■ Taking the Temperature:

Evaluate your marriage on a scale of 1-10 for each of the categories below. Write down your scores privately, and then discuss the differences in your perceptions and expectations about how your marriage is growing.

Each spouse: write your scores privately, and then share your scores with each other.

Hint: the point of the exercise is not the scores but the difference in perspective, expectations, and observations. The key component is: How will you work through the differences in your scores?

A score of 1 means there is no growth in this area.
A score of 10 means our marriage is perfect all the time in this area.

1. We pray together everyday.
2. We speak words of original design and blessing to each other every week.
3. We are not afraid to speak the truth in love to each other.
4. We agree on the biblical world view of one world-two realms.
5. We understand how sin and strongholds affect us, and pray with authority using the 4 R's.
6. We always speak tenderly and with honor to each other.

7. We are not afraid of each other's reactions.

8. Husband is initiating and leading the spiritual life of our marriage.

9. Wife is operating in peaceful partnership with husband in all things.

10. We see each other through the eyes of faith and hope, not fear or past history.

11. We have shared all our secrets and now live 100% in the light.

12. We have asked and received forgiveness for all offenses.

13. We have become unoffendable.

Once you have shared your scores with each other, talk and pray through any issues that may arise as a result of different perceptions or expectations surrounding the above topics.

Do not allow this exercise to be an opportunity for defeat, discouragement, shame, or division. Use it to identify areas that provide an opportunity for greater alignment in your marriage. Then take it out and do it again from time to time for maintenance and do a 30,000-, 60,000-, and 90,000-mile tune-up, just like you would for your car. You'll be glad you did!

ENDNOTES

1. A more thorough treatment of the teaching on "original design" can be found in *Living Free: Recovering God's Design for Your Life*, Mike Riches, Sycamore Publications, Gig Harbor, WA: 2008.

2. For more on this topic, see *Hearing God's Voice for Yourself and Others*, by Mike Riches and Tom Jonez, Sycamore Publications, Gig Harbor, WA: 2010.

3. Gingrich W. Arndt, F. W Danker, & W. Bauer (Editors). *A Greek-English Lexicon of the New Testament and other Early Christian Literature*, Chicago: University of Chicago Press, 1996, c1979, page 798.

4. Mike Riches, *Living Free: Recovering God's Design for Your Life*, Sycamore Publications, Gig Harbor, WA: 2008, page 20-22.

5. Illustration of the unforgiveness cycle adapted from the *Living Free Course*, Sycamore Publications.

6. Mike Riches, *Living Free Course Manual*, Sycamore Publications, Gig Harbor, WA: 2008, page 14.

7. unity. (n.d.). *The American Heritage® Dictionary of the English Language, Fourth Edition*. Retrieved November 25, 2008, from Dictionary.com website: http://dictionary.reference.com/browse/unity

8. For a more thorough teaching on "one-world, two-realms" see *Living Free: Recovering God's Original Design for Your Life*, Mike Riches, Sycamore Publications: Gig Harbor, WA, 2008.

9. I am grateful to Mike Riches for his contribution of the "octopus ink" material.

10. Mike Riches, *Living Free Course Manual*, Sycamore Publications, Gig Harbor, WA: 2008, page 39.

11.*Theological Dictionary of the New Testament* (10 vols.), G. Kittel, G. W. Bromiley & G. Friedrich, Ed. (Grand Rapids, Eerdmans 1964-c1976).

12. Mike Riches, *The Living Free Course Manual*, Sycamore Publications: 2008, Gig Harbor, WA page 39.

13. Arlyn Lawrence, from *A Heart Restored*, available 2011 from Sycamore Publications.

14. *American Heritage Dictionary*

15. *Words:* Edward Mote, *circa* 1834; first appeared in Mote's *Hymns of Praise*, 1836. *Music:* Solid Rock, William B. Bradbury, 1863 (MIDI, score)

16. Mike Riches, *The Living Free Course Manual*, Sycamore Publications: Gig Harbor, WA, 2008, page 81.

17. Ibid, page 73.

18. *The American Heritage® Dictionary of the English Language*, Fourth Edition, Houghton Mifflin Company: New York, New York, 2009.

19. For a more thorough treatment of learning to hear God's voice in prayer, I recommend the book *Hearing God's Voice for Yourself and Others* by Mike Riches and Tom Jonez, available from Sycamore Publications.

20. Stormie Omartian, *Lord, I Want to Be Whole*, Thomas Nelson Publishers: Nashville, TN, 2000, p. 43.

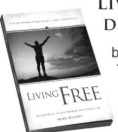

LIVING FREE COURSE
COMPLETE CURRICULUM KIT

This three-DVD set (six sessions) features the *Living Free* course taught live by author Mike Riches and includes course manual, leader's guide, and DVD course facilitator's guide.

HEARING GOD'S VOICE
FOR YOURSELF AND OTHERS

by Mike Riches and Tom Jonez
In this illustrated, full-color manual, you'll learn powerful truths and principles for returning to God's biblical normal for communicating with Him. Includes practical assignments for group or class study. Now available in German!

FREEDOM PRAYER
TRAINING MANUAL

COMING SPRING 2011!

Freedom prayer ministry is a powerful way to apply the biblical truths of *Living Free* and *Hearing God's Voice*. This training will equip you to help people encounter God's love and truth and be released into the freedom God designed for His children.